will they or won't they?

will they or won't they?

14 true stories
of adolescents finding faith

Ken Edgecombe

Scripture Union

Scripture Union books are published in Australia by
Scripture Union Resources for Ministry Unit
PO Box 77
Lidcombe
NSW 1825
Australia

And in the United Kingdom by
Scripture Union
207-209 Queensway
Bletchley, MK2 2EB
England

The National Library of Australia Cataloguing-in-Publication entry

Edgecombe, Ken, 1945- ..
Will they or won't they?: 14 true stories of adolescents
finding faith.

ISBN 0 949720 84 4.

1. Youth - Religious life. 2. Conversion - Christianity.
1. Title.

248.83

Cover and text design by Kelvin Young, Preston, Victoria
Printed and bound in Australia by Openbook Publishers, Adelaide

contents

introduction

In July 1994, the International Bulletin of Missionary Research published an article by Bryant L. Myers, Vice President for Mission and Evangelism for World Vision International and Director of Missions Advanced Research and Communication Centre. He was also Chairman of the Strategy Working Group of the Lausanne Committee for World Evangelisation at the time. He had impressive credentials.

Myers reproduced a graph from Lionel Hunt's Handbook on Child Evangelism (Chicago: Moody Press, 1960) entitled 'Ages at Which People Become Christians'. This graph told us that 1 per cent of people who become Christians do so before the age of four, 10 per cent between the ages of 15 and 30, and 4 per cent after the age of 30. The rest, adding up to 85 per cent, do so between the ages of 4 and 14 years.

That's a lot of Christians in a single age group. You might imagine, as a consequence, that churches would therefore put 85 per cent of their effort into that age group, capitalising on the trend. But you would be wrong - they don't. Not only do churches not put most of their resources into this age group, but many fail to put any resources there at all. Few churches have specialist children's workers. Traditionally, Bible College classes on children's ministries fail to attract large numbers of students. Often, if children are given biblical teaching, it is taught in sub-standard church facilities. Their teachers are often rostered to the job, have little training and use out-dated methods of imparting knowledge. There is little evidence of any comprehensive plan by churches for an all-out assault geared to maximise the impact of ministering to this age group.

So how do such people, between the ages of 4 and 14, come to faith at all? You may well ask. This book does not supply all the answers but it does listen to the stories of fourteen such young people - people who became Christians between the ages of 10 and 14. How was it for these young people? What was their pathway? What are the common threads?

So far as fourteen people may form a survey, these pages are that survey. How we grapple with its results is up to us to decide.

acknowledgments

Anyone who sits down at one end of the world to compile a book about people from the other end of the world and from points in between, is reliant on the help and co-operation of many people. I would like to publicly express my appreciation to Clayton Fergie, David Goold, Terry and Shona Cobham, Michael Hews, Chen Cheng Mok, Gary Colville, Jenny Hyatt, Phil Lindsay and Janet Berkovic who put me in touch with some of my subjects, and to Terry and Shona, Jenny and Janet for their on-going liaison and interviewing work. Tricia Fountain and Viv Whitford spent hours at a word processor. John and Rosemary Russell, Sue Bluett and Linda van Leeuwen all did some prospecting for subjects, and Paul Clark offered to submit a chapter.

Fourteen people have agreed to make their stories public, and members of their families have contributed in various ways. So have mine. John Lane provided the initial germ of an idea, and his intermittent encouragement and advice has seen the germ grow into viral proportions. Rena Pritchard and Daniel Batt have sorted me out editorially in a hundred ways. God has reminded me that he is in charge of the process I have tried to describe.

To them all, and to others: thank you.

K.J Edgecombe Wellington, New Zealand

unlikely origins

Graham Eagle

Graham Eagle might drive a Range Rover, own a packaging firm with many overseas contacts and live in a comfortable house in the town of Napier in Hawkes Bay, New Zealand. But he takes none of the comfort of his current existence for granted. After a painful and fragmented childhood, he believes the fact that he made the most of the opportunities presented to him (while others he knew didn't), is evidence of something other than his own wisdom and industry. Graham, now in his fifties, is one who found faith as an adolescent.

When he first saw his birth certificate at the age of 41, Graham looked to the section headed 'father'. There were four blank spaces.

He was brought up first by his grandfather, then later by various combinations of an aunt and uncle, his grandmother, mother and a stepfather. He still does not know who his father was. His mother used to spend a lot of time with the sailors who passed through the Napier port in the 1940s, and one of these men appears to have fathered a child he may never have known about. Graham took his surname from Ivor Eagle, the man his mother married in her late teens.

Graham's family is as elusive as his sailor father. He grew up with his brother, Ron, two years older. He rarely saw Ivor, another older brother, who died of a heart attack in Australia when he was 53. When aged 28, Graham met for the first time two much older sisters. He also has a half brother nearby whom he has never met. One sister always felt there was something missing in her life, someone once close. She finally tracked down her twin sister in adulthood, only to discover she had the mentality of a child. Her twin had been taken away by the Social Welfare Department because of the family's alcoholism and violence. Graham is not sure how many other half-brothers or sisters there are, since no one has ever brought them all together.

Graham participates in the leadership of his church and is a successful business and family man. His wife Linda and their children, Nicky, Karen, Natasha and Jane, have brought him a profound sense of fulfilment. Yet the present doesn't annul the past. 'I've always struggled with self-confidence,' Graham says, as he remembers the pain and embarrassment of his childhood.

'My grandfather was everything in those early years,' he says. 'His own marriage had broken up and he looked after Ron and me on his own.' Graham saw his mother irregularly and as a child, wasn't sure just how she fitted into things. 'She used to work the night shift and she had her own idea of a social life. My sisters used to come across her, often drunk, at parties when they were at high school. It was embarrassing for them.'

As Graham looks back he can see that to others, his grandfather might not have seemed the most responsible carer. 'To anyone looking on, my grandfather would not have looked too wonderful-he used to fossick around the local rubbish dump to add to his pension. But he was wonderful to me. He established my first ideas of love and basic trust, and my early values. He was there for me.'

One Christmas, the reality of society's hierarchy of privilege suddenly dawned on him. 'I was five when I realised we were very poor. I had no idea at all about Christmas. Ron told me about how people gave each other presents. And I cried because none of that fitted us.' When his grandfather discovered Graham crying, he opened his pension packet and gave the boys half a crown each. 'Twenty-five cents in today's currency doesn't sound much, but five shillings must have been a lot of money for my Grandad in 1952. I'd never had so much money in my life-I spent it all on an enormous bag of sweets.'

Graham remembers that it was about this time, when he was six, that the Social Welfare department realised he was not attending school and sent someone to ensure he went back. 'I must have been reluctant about schools. I remember my grandfather sent me to a Sunday School once, but I ran away after about 10 minutes. He didn't make me go back. Ordinary school was a little more successful for me, in that I eventually went to it.'

But much worse things were to happen. 'My grandad died that year. I was devastated. He died of tetanus, picked up at the rubbish tip. And when the reality of death entered my life, I cried out instinctively to another reality whose name I never remember having heard. "Oh God," I said, "Grandad's dead. Who's going to look after me now?" '

His aunt and uncle (his mother's brother) stepped in. 'They didn't want us to be with them,' he says, 'but my grandfather had made my uncle promise that we would not have to go into a home, like our sisters. We didn't really like it at my uncle's. They'd wave the Family Benefit book at us from time to time and say, "Your mother hasn't paid this." It meant you were always clear that they were doing you a favour and guilty about the trouble you were causing. But that was home for the next six or seven years.'

At about the age of 12 or 13, Graham and Ron moved to Masterton, in the south east of the North Island. They stayed with their grandmother, their grandfather's ex-wife. Her husband had recently died, so she wanted the family to come and help with the farm. It was a miserable year for the boys, helping with farm chores for a woman they never really knew. As Graham and Ron discovered another part of the family, they also discovered more family tragedies. 'She had run away from my grandfather years before,' Graham recalls, 'and I found out later that he had spent all his savings trying to find out where she was. She moved in with this other man and took his name, though I don't think they ever married. My grandfather never did find her.'

The boys' grandmother did not provide the nurture and love they had always lacked. Grief, and perhaps the pain of the past, prevented her from ever being able to relate to her grandsons.

However, one event shook Graham up in a most unexpected way. The local Seventh Day Adventist pastor came knocking on the door and the boys' grandmother invited him in, in the hope that he might be able to scare some cooperation into them. 'He gave us a whole presentation, with slides and all sorts of things, mostly about the righteous judgment of God and the dangers of hell,' Graham says. 'I was scared. The fear of it all caused me to go to his church when he invited us. We had no idea about churches. He just said to us, "Wear your best." '

The boys turned up regularly during that year. From time to time, the pastor would invite anyone present to make a public decision to follow Jesus, and Graham responded to one of these. Though he looks back on the decision as perhaps manipulated and mostly based on fear, yet his admiration of the lives of his friends at the church provided both a safe environment for the decision and a type of relationship he had never experienced.

'I had never seen people like this. It was my first contact with people who showed love on a widespread scale, and it attracted me. You could see Jesus in the way these people related to one another. I had then-and in many ways still have-difficulty in feeling some of the Christian truths that my head understands more easily.'

Graham's mother re-married that year and the boys came back to Napier to live with her and their new stepfather. Graham was due to start at Napier Boys' High School, a place he still sees as especially significant 40 years on.

An architect called Martin Yeoman lived in Napier, a faithful leader of the Christian group meeting at the High School. When Graham Eagle enrolled at school, he received a letter from Martin Yeoman on behalf of the 'Crusaders' (known later as the Inter-School Christian Fellowship, ISCF). Martin wrote to every new third former as he had struck up a good relationship with the principal, who gave him the addresses of all new enrolments.

'The timing for me was just right,' Graham says. 'I had just left the Seventh Day Adventist Church in Masterton and we had not linked up with the Adventists in Napier. Mum didn't like the idea, but she said we could go along there if we wanted to. Her idea of church was that you went to a different church every week-you walked in the door and you walked out. You didn't get involved. As a "home kid" in her second hand shoes and clothes, she was used to the general ridicule of society.

'The Crusaders' program wasn't any big drama, or even exciting. There would be a group of around 12 to 20 boys. Martin would give a talk from the front with his little pocket Bible. He might show us a Moody science film-we enjoyed those. I always used to go, and I'd say to my friends, "Hey, it's Wednesday. Let's go". They often did.'

As well as the school groups, Martin organised a number of camps and 'tramps', or hikes, in the mountains. For Graham, these were an adventure, and not just in physical terms. 'It was a lifeline,' he recalls with joy. 'They happened maybe three or four times a year, and I loved it. The fellowship and the singing and the sheer health and beauty of it all-all in such contrast to everything I was used to. I worked part-time in the market gardens and the money I earned meant I could attend Crusader camps in the school holidays. I got seriously into this tramping kind of life; the environment and Christian fellowship were life to me.'

There have been many times over the years when Graham has wondered how a man can be so effective, just standing up the front with a little pocket Bible. He sees that the gentle yet unpredictable Spirit of God appears to have been working through Martin and in his own life. He remembers the misery of his home life and wonders why other members of his own family met similar contrasts with quite different responses. Graham says simply that the Spirit placed an appetite for God within him. He was searching for something, and this is where he found it.

Those contrasts between the crusader camps and home are something Graham can never forget. 'We'd come back home to the fights and the booze, and life was hell. I was at high school for three and a half years, and all that time this contrast was clearly in front of me. I decided that I did not want the life I was seeing at home. I remember my oldest brother, Ivor, coming home once when he was about 18 or 19. He had a job at Waipukurau, just south of Napier, and he came to stay with us. When he saw the violence and the effects of the drink, he said to me, "I'll never come back to this house again." He never did. He left for Australia not long afterwards and lived there until he died. He did come back to Napier two or three times but he used to book in at a motel.

'It's a frightening thing, when you're 16, hearing your mother being beaten up in the next room. She often had a cut face or black eyes. We used to try to go to the movies at night, staying out till one o'clock, hoping they'd be asleep when we got home.

I was conscious of being a Christian by the time I was 16, because of the Crusader group, and I remember praying, "God, take the booze out of our lives." '

This prayer was not unlike that cry to God after he learned his grandfather had died, a phrase repeated around the world thousands of times every day, yet so many people never seem to experience an answer. However, within twelve months, Graham's mother and stepfather had given up the drink completely.

'A funny little thing led to it,' he recalls. 'It was in the days of 6 o'clock closing. The hotel's doors shut at six, but those who knew the ropes could work the system after that. My mother and stepfather went over there one day-they'd been going there for years-and the publican wouldn't let them in. They were amazed, and angry too. They looked at his car in the yard and they said, "Who paid for that? We did. Well, that's that. He can keep it. Finish."

'It was amazing-they gave up the drink. Just like that. Things improved at home considerably after that, but I never did get on well with my stepfather, who didn't really want me there. He seemed more accepting of Ron, I always thought. But I finally understood why when I found out later that he was actually Ron's father.'

Graham traces the earliest hints of God's presence in his life to his grandfather. 'He had these autograph books, and he used to write a lot of poetry in them-just for himself. He certainly wasn't a poet, he was actually a champion axeman, but I used to read his poems, and all through them were references to God and the mountains. Just from reading them, you got the sense that he knew something about God, and about pain. And when I was at high school, I found God, and the mountains.

'You can't tell what's come down to you through your parents, or through theirs. I found out not long ago that Grandad's father was an Anglican minister. He got into all sorts of moral trouble and his marriage broke up. He was a wayward guy. Then later, my grandfather's marriage broke up, and my mother's.'

For Graham's generation, though, even with all of that history to contend with, not one marriage has broken up, and none of them even drink. Yet no one else has become a Christian either.

No marriage stays together on its own and Graham has had plenty of struggles that a simple prayer won't fix. 'I often thought of my parents' struggles with marriage, and my grandparents', and I'd think my marriage was going to go too. I said so to myself and to Linda. It was like a curse on me. But it didn't go. I attribute that to the love of Linda and to the grace of God. It's possible to look at people in the church and to think they've got everything together. But everyone makes mistakes. We need to foster a climate that makes it possible to talk about them, so we can help each other.'

Be that as it may, their marriage has grown through those early, difficult years. Graham emerged from childhood with a lot of anger, and it stayed with him for a long time. When he married, he was on medication for depression, nervous tension and mental blanks, and he feared having a mental breakdown. He had a 'lone ranger' approach to life as well-he had always done his own thing and had not developed the habit of discussing what he was doing with anyone. He suffered from depression and stress. None of these things are calculated to make either marriage or fatherhood easy.

But Graham has worked hard at whatever was his to do. During his last years of living with his mother before he married, he saved enough to buy land and to put down a deposit to build a house. When they married and moved into this new home, Linda's savings furnished it. Graham continued to work hard and there were times when his business became first an outlet, then an unhealthy obsession, working there for long hours in the evenings and at weekends. It became an escape from the need to face personal relationship issues. 'I had to learn that if God does not make the business go, I can't either. I had to turn things over to him and face my other responsibilities.'

Graham's journey is not over. A casual observer might say he has made it, but his development and growth go on. As he looks back, Graham Eagle ponders the mystery of why he responded to those early messages of Christianity while others of his family did not; why much of the tragedy of his parents' generation didn't flow through into his own. While it may seem that he has made the most of his opportunities, Graham sees that it is God who is trying to make the most of him. And God did it through those who told him of Jesus, faithfully and consistently, at a time when those at home were not in a position to offer him anything.

well, what made the difference?

Apart from the faithful telling of the Seventh Day Adventist pastor and Crusader leader, Graham sees several influences in his spiritual journey.

1. From his grandfather he learned love and basic trust, which some say are essential before a person can find faith. While it's often in adolescence that young people first profess faith, the foundations are set up much earlier. What more could we do in our homes and churches to provide this basis for children?

2. Graham started going to church when an itinerant pastor spoke of God's righteous judgment and hell. Is that message part of the gospel we live and present to young people? Should it be? In what contexts did Jesus speak of such things?

3. Martin Yeoman appears to have had a powerful yet simple message and way of operating. He sought out new contacts. He 'talked' the Christian message regularly. He arranged camps and adventure times. His activities were not spectacular, but they had lasting impact. What does this say about what is effective in ministry?

kept by the power of God

Annette Bailey

When she was in her early 20s, Annette Bailey nearly gave up on God entirely. While working in country New South Wales as a relief nurse for a mission society, she found the hypocrisy among some of the people she encountered shattering to her Christian faith.

It was the early 1960s and she found the people she worked with had developed a set of rules for who would be the right sorts of people for her to befriend. One local woman who wore no make-up and played the church piano was 'acceptable' although Annette found her to be the cruellest gossip. Friendships with members from another church in the area were forbidden because the church occasionally screened films for station workers on a hotel wall and organised some dances. Annette was stunned by the legalism applied first to these people and then to her. Instead of friendship and a Christianity of love, all Annette found were cold people obsessed with formality and rules.

It nearly destroyed her. She came back to the city, enrolled to do her Midwifery Certificate and said to God, 'I want 12 months off, with you not in my life, because I don't like the people who call themselves yours.'

But Annette's story begins many years before this event. She was born in 1942, the youngest of a family of five, 15 years younger than her oldest sister, and three years younger than her next oldest brother. After being ill for many years, her father died at 47, shortly before her seventh birthday. Stomach cancer, linked to wounds he had received in World War 1, finally took its toll.

Annette grew up in the immediate post-war years in Regents Park, a suburb in the west of Sydney. Then it was new, and way, way out west. It was also poor, designed and built by the Housing Commission especially for war widows and those on war pensions. There were four styles of houses and four colours-duck egg blue, green, pink and yellow. The houses were painted in order, the sequence then repeated. Annette's house was duck egg blue.

The gravel roads through the suburb created a fine dust in the dry and thick mud in the wet. There were very few trees and hardly any grass. Many people grew potatoes where later there would be front lawns. Blackberries grew profusely-Annette's family had a backyard full of them-and they slowly dealt with them over the next few years, by grubbing and spraying.

Annette considered her family lucky, because their house was on the fringe of the suburb, next to the dairy farm from which the sub-division had been created, and they could go and see the dairy cows from time to time. This was exciting for them, because as a rule they did not go anywhere. Every year, they saved up to travel across the city to Manly Beach to see the sea.

In the years just after the war, a man called a rabbit-oh used to come around from street to street, selling rabbits. The iceman delivered ice for their ice chests and the dunny man came once a week to empty the toilet can.

Annette has strong images of walking once a week to the Housing Commission pay office to queue to pay the rent, and of the family's struggle to pay it. She also has sharp memories of families evicted for failing to pay. Her mother struggled to provide uniforms for her two remaining school children. There were four of them in the house, Annette, her older sister who was now working, her brother and her mother. Her oldest sister had married and the other brother, when he was 14, went to become a jackeroo, an apprentice on a sheep station.

Annette was nine when the family moved into the Regents Park house. Before that, they lived for two years in a little flat above a shop in Leichhardt. After her father died they were thrown out of the house in Russell Lea where she was born. Thinking back, Annette recalls that the most positive aspect of her life through those times was school.

'I did well there,' she says. 'I was a reasonably keen student, with a good head and I felt affirmed and loved there. When we were moving from the flat to Regents Park, I looked forward to the new school, I loved going there and was very happy.

'In Christian terms, my early education was pretty spasmodic. My mother had been brought up in Wales, in a very strict Church of England tradition in which she went to church on Sunday morning, sat in the parlour on Sunday afternoon and then went to Evensong. The parlour time had strict rules of behaviour-she could read the Bible or "The Pilgrim's Progress", but nothing secular. She could do her cross-stitch but not her mending-mending was work. It was a pretty joyless sort of outlook and my mother determined that her children were not going to be subjected to that kind of upbringing. Consequently, we only went to church on rare occasions.'

Annette doesn't believe that her mother lost sight of God. It was just that she didn't feel she had been well served by the practices of which she had been a part. For her, faith was very personal and she was suspicious of those who spoke easily of 'being a Christian'. This sounded to her like presumption upon a God who was holy and mighty and more than somewhat inscrutable. 'She probably prayed throughout her life,' Annette recalls. 'But she would never have talked about it.'

As an infant, before her father died, Annette was baptised and that gave her a pair of godparents who became part of her spiritual journey. 'My mother was happy to allow me to go to

Sunday School and I went for a while, irregularly. While we were living in the flat when I was eight or nine, someone invited me to Christian Endeavour. That's an interdenominational organisation, still operating in Australia, which has the aim of training leaders in the Christian faith. I've forgotten who asked me but I caught the tram up the hill and went regularly for about eight months before the family moved to Regents Park. It was very precious. When we had moved, I remember asking if I could go to Sunday School, but it wasn't easy. There wasn't even a church in our area and it was very difficult to go to the next suburb. Someone from my school used to go and they took me occasionally.'

When Annette was nearly 11, the Sydney Anglican Diocese established a 'mobile church' in Regents Park. The mobile church was a relocatable building placed on a vacant piece of land and bolted to a prelaid foundation. It could be moved to another place where a church was required. The minister had charge of a number of churches in the neighbourhood. A spartan building, it had none of the fittings associated with conventional churches such as books or a piano. No one else in Annette's family was inclined to walk the two-mile return journey to attend. But from the time the church arrived, Annette went regularly to Sunday School.

'I never remember feeling deprived by the humble nature of the church,' she says. 'The one in the next suburb was a grand affair, with an organ and stained glass windows and all the rest of it, but it didn't seem to matter. It was just so exciting to actually have a church in our suburb. The Catholics were building one as well, a much grander place and I guess we were a bit envious about it. But in Sydney in the early 1950s there was a lot of Catholic/Anglican rivalry, even conflict, and us kids certainly caught it. So we became very proud of our little church, in a fit of some sort of reverse snobbery.'

Annette's godparents gave her a Bible and Christian books, and from time to time invited her to church. They worshipped at a Presbyterian church, which to Annette seemed quite strange. 'Their style was different from anything I knew. But they were praying people. They tried to help me to understand God, in little ways, on my visits there-they always said grace at meals, for example. We never did at home. It was their way and I knew that God was, somehow, part of their home.'

Annette sees her main Christian influence coming through her religious education at school. 'When I look back,' she recalls, 'I'm sure the headmaster was a Christian and that's why he had such a good influence on the school and on me. He taught me the basic moral teachings of Christianity without calling them that.'

Annette cannot give a set date for becoming a Christian. When she was aged about 13 she attended her first Inter-School Christian Fellowship camp. There she envied people who could set such a date. 'Everyone else seemed to have a "spiritual birthday". I had none and I was most upset about it.'

During Grade 4, a former missionary in China visited her Religious Education class. She drew on the blackboard the Chinese character for 'come', which looks very much like the figure of Christ on the cross. She said that, even in the ancient culture of China, and it is not even known whether Christianity went there, the words symbolised what the gospel meant. She said to the class: 'That's what Jesus is saying to you now- "Come" '. And Annette walked home from school saying, 'Yes, Lord Jesus, I want you to come into my life.'

'It wasn't the end of my "conversion experience" but it was a significant step for me. I felt at home in my Sunday School afterwards, as if I belonged. I knew, absolutely somehow, that God was my father and that he was not going to die or otherwise go and leave me. I don't know how I knew, but it was part of me and I knew.'

Nothing memorable occurred in Annette's journey for the next couple of years, until she was 12 and at Parramatta High School. She went there prepared to be identified as a Christian, joining the Inter-School Christian Fellowship (ISCF) group, where there were many discussions over how to relate to God.

Soon after starting high school, as Annette was walking from the branch church to the church at Regents Park, the new minister asked her directly, whether or not she was a Christian. 'As I attempted to answer him, the understanding dawned on me that the initial step towards God had never been updated. I tracked him down again in the days following and he said to me, 'Are you sure you're a Christian?' I said, 'No, I'm not. I just know that I love God and that he loves me, and that Jesus is my friend.' Looking back, it wasn't bad but I think for the first time then, I actually heard the steps of salvation explained. I said to him, 'Well, I've done most of that,' and he said, "You have too. I think you're a Christian." '

Most of Annette's friends from the Anglican church were being confirmed at around 12 years of age. But she didn't feel ready to make a public statement. She explains: 'It was because my mother would have come to the service and maybe others would have, too. And if she came and witnessed my confirmation, she would be able to say, "Well, excuse me, but why don't you keep your room tidy? And why don't you stop arguing with your brother? And why don't you do a lot of other things?" '

'In fact, for a couple of years at high school, I lived a sort of double life. I got involved in a lot of Christian things at school and church and became something of a leader at the ISCF. But I hadn't let my faith change me at home very much. It's the opposite of what a lot of kids from Christian homes experience. A lot of them are Christian at home, but not at school. For me it took a while to catch on at home, where I still had arguments with my sister and brother and I treated my mother less than well.'

One day, just before her 14th birthday, Annette's godmother spoke with her about the importance of a public statement of one's Christian faith. Her godmother helped Annette to see that she didn't have to live the consistent Christian life before publicly owning her faith. She had been trying to 'do a lot in my own strength' and came to see that God had already made her able. She was confirmed soon after.

'It was about the same time that I went on an ISCF camp and someone told me I was playing games with God, not serious about him being Lord of my life, because I wasn't really prepared to sacrifice absolutely everything for him. I was very challenged by this. I went home and I thought about it a lot and realised it was true. God was my father and he was precious to me, but I wanted him on my terms. The giving was all God's, not mine. I went through a period of submitting, of acknowledging that God had the right to do anything he chose with my life, and of consciously giving him the reins.'

By the time she was 15, Annette had decided she would commit herself to a life of full-time Christian service. She began to put this commitment into practice, as far as a 15 year old is able. She joined the League of Youth, the young people's department of the Church Missionary Society, and served on various mission teams to local churches. She taught in Sunday School, maintained her ISCF links and commenced some theological studies. In 1960, aged 18, she left home and went to Melbourne to do nursing training, conscious that it would prepare her for missionary service. By then, she had also completed the Sydney preliminary theological course.

'It would be a mistake to suggest it all became a clear course forward,' Annette warns. 'I had been decisively disobedient to God in walking out of High School during the June of my last year and, in doing so, blowing any chance there may have been of going to a university. This at a time when I believed God was calling me to be a teacher. So nursing was only a next best. But I worked for a year for a missionary society and then did three nursing certificates.'

Some time later, Annette felt God had some purpose for her in Darwin. For 18 months after leaving school she had done office work for the Bush Church Aid Society (BCA). So, when Carpentaria College, an Anglican college providing residential care for remote settlement children, asked BCA to supply a nurse to the College, Annette responded.

That was over 30 years ago, and Annette is still in Darwin. A year after arriving there she met Graham Bailey, a town planner. They were married in 1970, not long before she turned 29. Today, Annette is the mother of three and a grandmother as well. She has taught religious education in schools in Darwin for many years-a task she feels passionate about-and has worked in various ways with Scripture Union in the Northern Territory since 1968. She has recently been ordained as a deacon to work with St Peter's Anglican church in Darwin. Currently she is the Pastoral care Worker for the Palliative care Team at the Public Hospital in Darwin.

Annette sees clear links between the Christian work she has done as an adult and the Christian experiences she had as a child. She gives great credit to a deaconess attached to her parish just after the war, who taught Religious Education in school and visited homes also, as part of her church duties. Annette figures it highly likely that this woman's visit to her mother paved the way for her own attendance at Sunday School, to say nothing of the value of the RE lessons she experienced at school. The ISCF camps she attended through her High School years benefited her enormously because this was where she learned to pray. She discovered there the discipline of regular, solitary prayer to God and also the thrill of seeing group prayers answered.

She reflects that she has never been coerced or blackmailed into any significant Christian response, but has always been allowed to take away the knowledge of the moment, think about it, pray about it and make a commitment in her own time. She recalls that her faith was allowed to mature along with her, commitment growing as her understanding developed.

Annette recognises that she would be in a very different place today without the Christian input of those early years. She recalls her crisis of faith in the early 1960s and remembers thinking at the time that without God, she had nothing. And she couldn't have God without his people. The church may not be immune from the prejudices of society but its future lies with those, like Annette, who make it their life's goal to take the love of God wherever they can.

well, what made the difference?

Annette Bailey unexpectedly grew to faith in childhood, even though she did not grow up in a Christian context. What can we learn from the numerous Christian influences on her life?

1. Annette's school headmaster created a caring, teaching atmosphere that reinforced her inclinations to do well. What have been the inspiring schoolteachers or headmasters who have influenced you most for the good? What about teachers in a church or RE context? What characteristics did they display and which of these characteristics do you think are most helpful in bringing young people to faith?

2. Many around Annette challenged her to a high level of Christian commitment. How can this be done without it becoming elitist and making people feel they haven't made the grade?

3. For some time, Annette felt her Christian life at home prevented her from being confirmed. Can there be a level of inconsistency in a person's Christianity that should prevent their making a public statement of faith? What is the best way to challenge the young people we know in this area?

arguing with priests

Rene Galbes

As a teenager, when Rene Galbes discovered his mother secretly putting powder from the local occultist in his coffee, he knew that becoming a Christian would not be as simple as just changing his taste in music. He had discovered a way of life that required a deep commitment, one that might cost him his relationship with his family. But Rene was used to making decisions for himself amid the seedy street life of Marseille in the 1960s.

Rene was three years old when his family migrated to France from Morocco in 1954. His father had worked in a lead mine before he left for Marseille in search of work. This big family of Spanish origins settled in La Capelette, a working class quarter of the inner city.

Marseille is the second largest city in France. It is situated on the southern French Mediterranean coast. Founded around 600 BC by Phoenician sailors as a trading and fishing port, it has been a major trading point ever since, between Africa, the Middle East and Europe. Its population is a vibrant mix of cultures, the result of centuries of immigration from countries around the Mediterranean seaboard. There has been a major influx of immigrants from North Africa since World War II, as Marseille is the closest port to the motherland for citizens of the former French Empire, who come looking for work and a new start in life. The Arab quarter of Marseille is full of colour and movement, with open stalls on the footpaths and small shops spilling out of doorways.

The religious traditions of Marseille are as diverse as its people. France, traditionally a Roman Catholic country, has been a secular state since its Revolution in the 18th century. In theory, no religion is favoured and all may practise their religion with freedom. Marseille has variously been home to Greek and Roman temples, Jewish synagogues, monumental Catholic churches, Moslem mosques, as well as other religions brought by the migrant populations. It still is. During the 1950s and '60s when Rene was growing up, he remembers his family as 'Catholic, non-practising'-not involved in the church, but holding on to its religious roots. They were very superstitious, something he attributes to their Spanish background and Latin temperament. His family visited fortune-tellers and regularly participated in other folk and occult practices.

Rene's upbringing was not sheltered from Marseille's street life. 'I wouldn't say I was brought up in the street,' he says, 'but I was often there, and I met all sorts of people. And because we came from such a big family, each of us had to find our own way very, very young.' For 'all sorts' of people, read exactly that-this is a working class, cosmopolitan French port. It is a compact place-a million plus people housed among vast white rock cliffs, with buildings growing out of rock faces and the sea open to Spain and Africa.

Marseille doesn't have a strong Christian presence. The most noticeable features of Christendom are the large buildings of the Catholic church. The Cathedral of Nôtre Dame de la Garde's hilltop aspect commands the city so centrally that it became the centre of the German resistance during the 1944 battle for Marseille. The building's exterior still bears the scars of the battle, while its interior bears the marks of the local seafarers' reverence to Mary, for ocean voyages safely completed.

In the Galbes family, it was traditional for each child to take their first communion and join the Catholic Church. Rene began his catechism classes while at primary school. But he had his adolescent crisis of faith when he was about 13, and the Church came in for its share of his questioning.

'I was actually quite mature for my age-the result of a fair measure of imposed independence that stemmed from a large family and preoccupied parents. I had the capacity to reason about some of the fundamental questions of life. I did not share these questions with either of my parents. My father was seldom at the house because of his job. He worked very hard as a building site foreman and when he came home at night he was tired and ready for bed. My mother who was at home, could neither read nor write.'

But Rene shared the results of his questioning with his mother. 'One day I said to my mother, 'I don't want to go to catechism any more.' She simply said, 'In our family, everyone does their first communion. That's how it is. You'll do yours like all the rest.' So I finished the course, but I wasn't convinced. I remember the day of my first communion very clearly. Like all the other candidates, I entered the church in the communion procession wearing all the appropriate robes, but as I looked towards the altar I said-and I don't know who to-'God doesn't exist.' It was my first clear statement of what I had been coming to believe over quite a period.'

After communion, Rene decided that he was an atheist. It was the sort of independent stance he was accustomed to taking. But he didn't just disbelieve in God, he was angry at the whole idea of God. Although usually polite with his parents, the merest mention of God was enough to make him lose control. His mother often quoted a popular saying, 'si Dieu le veut'-literally, 'if it is God's will'-which she employed without reflection. It made Rene angry and he remembers responding on one occasion: 'God! We can't even see him, so don't speak about him.'

This questioning soon turned into a smouldering anger. At school he refused to work and he had no desire to achieve anything. After many futile attempts to get him to become more co-operative, the authorities eventually kicked him out of school. Soon after, Rene failed his tests to begin a panel-beating apprenticeship, and his future wasn't looking good.

But just when he might have simply drifted into the illicit street life of Marseille, Rene got talking to a friend who had been in a similar situation a year or two before. 'He told me it wasn't too late,' Rene recalls. 'There were good private schools that gave second chances to people like me. He told me that I should find one and try to work there, and he offered to help me with the lessons.'

When he went to the headmaster of one of these schools and told him he wanted to enrol, the headmaster asked him where his parents were. 'I told him my father was at work and my mother couldn't read or write. So there I was. I had become quite used to organising my own life.'

The French government, through social welfare, paid for this private Catholic school's fees, because Rene came from a large, poor family. Like most of the Catholic schools at the time, there was a priest attached to the school as a chaplain.

Rene didn't hold back in the religious discussions and remembers once saying to this priest: 'You're always speaking of heaven, when it's not even logical. The earth is round and we don't even know what's up or down. So how can we know where heaven is?' However, the priest acknowledged that Rene's criticism was understandable. He became interested in him through these questions and invited Rene to talk with him further. After covering a variety of topics, he then asked, 'Have you ever read the Bible?'

Rene's answer was no. Even though he had done his catechism, received his first communion and inherited a form of Catholic practice from his family, he had absolutely no idea what the Bible was. 'There were no Bibles at our place. My mother couldn't have read one if there were and my father was never home.' He recalls the priest saying that it was 'a book that must be read'. He lent me one-a very big, heavy, church Bible, which I carried the two kilometres home.

'I began to read this Bible, starting from the beginning. But I didn't understand much of it and went back to the priest to ask him what it all meant. Although he gave me some superficial help, he really only explained the meaning of the words, not the message they conveyed.'

Rene carried on with the task for around six months when one day, as he was carrying the big Bible home from the priest, he ran into the friend helping him with school. Seeing the big book in his hands, his friend grabbed it from him and began to flick through the pages. 'What have you got here?' he asked. 'A Bible? Whatever are you carrying this around for?' 'I've been talking to the priest about it,' Rene explained. 'He said I ought to read it, so he's lent me one.'

'And are you reading it? I wouldn't have thought you'd have a lot of time for that sort of thing. What do you think of it?'

If Rene had been honest, he would have said he didn't really think very much at all, because he still couldn't understand anything except at the shallowest level. But he didn't want to say that. So he ended up muttering that he thought he was more in agreement with the Protestants than the Catholics, and that he couldn't reconcile the Bible with the Catholic religion.

'So far as it went, it was true. I was perturbed by questions like why priests couldn't marry. I wanted to know the reasons behind all the traditions of the Catholic Church. There seemed to be a lot of things that I couldn't link back to the Bible, not even the little of it that I knew. When I asked questions at home, the answers all boiled down to 'Because that's the way it is.' This blind acceptance of authority in the status quo was the last thing I wanted. What the priests taught at school, and wherever else I heard them, didn't seem to relate at all to what happened at home. There seemed to be a big gap between religion and life, or between what the church seemed to be on about and what happened where you lived. As well as all that, I had some fundamental questions, like creation: How did we get here? Did we have a purpose? What did the Bible say about these things and what were the priests saying?'

Rene genuinely wondered about these questions and told his friend he would love to understand the Bible, if it had anything to say to these questions. 'He offered to take me to a place where they studied the Bible. It turned out to be a church he was attending, L'Église Libre de Alle Gambetta. I found out later that he was a Christian and he was beginning to see that perhaps he could help me towards God, too.

'In reality, an evolution had been going on in my life over several months. I had progressed from blind rebellion and atheism to the point of saying that, even though all I knew of religion did not satisfy me, God must have existed somewhere because of the evidence of creation. It seemed to me that the pattern and balance of the world, the complexity and diversity of it and its intricate detail, all pointed to a rational mind somewhere.'

At about the same time as he was doing this thinking, Rene met some Mormons. They came to his home in the course of their door-to-door visitation program. He talked to them and they invited him to their meetings. He was interested enough to go along for several months, although he never believed their teaching. But his very attendance revealed a person a long way removed from the boy who couldn't bear to hear his mother repeating casually, 'si Dieu le veut', just a matter of months before.

He also made friends with a local tradesman, a mattress-maker. They had long discussions on all sorts of topics. The man was a Protestant, a member of the French Reformed Church and one day he introduced Rene to his pastor. The two talked together for hours and by now the question of God had been resolved. 'I had begun to believe in God, but I didn't know anything more. I was ready to begin my path towards God and I was prepared to go somewhere where they could explain the Bible to me.

'It was at this stage that my friend from school took me along to his evangelical church in the centre of town. I began to attend the meetings there and I was happy enough just to do that for several months, although there was no change to my beliefs during that time. But one thing struck me. The first time I met the pastor, he said to me, "Ah, Rene. Your name is Rene but you must be reborn." In French, this is a play on words-the verb "renaître" means "reborn".'

Rene didn't understand what he was saying but he replied without really thinking that he would like to be. Some time later, when they were talking, the pastor said seriously, Rene, 'I want to tell you that Jesus died for you. He loves you and he died on the cross to save you.'

'I had never heard that in such a clear way before,' he recalls. 'At this moment, I had no more doubts. I can't explain why-he didn't convince me through an argument or anything like that. I just knew within me. Accustomed as I was to argument and debate, I tried to understand it and to reason out what was happening. But at the moment of my realisation or acceptance, I found I had nothing at all to say. Instead, I felt deep down inside myself that it was all true. When he asked me if I believed, I answered yes.'

Rene, who had never prayed before, got down on his knees with the pastor and prayed for God to come into his life. The pastor explained to him that he had become a Christian-not a Protestant but a Christian.

'I can say that I was completely new. I had finally understood the message of Jesus' sacrifice. Some people have progressive conversions and my own was confirmed over the years, but I believe that the Holy Spirit visited me and that I was reborn in that instant. I was a completely changed boy. I even began to work at school-it was as if God made me able to understand my lessons and to apply myself.'

Suddenly, as he read the Bible, at last it started to make sense. He soon started Bible studies at home with his elder brother and sister, and three younger sisters who all became interested in what had happened to him. He even told his father that he had experienced something that had satisfied him-and it was not the Catholic religion he had been taught during catechism. 'I told him that I didn't want to be Catholic any more,' Rene says. 'His response was that these were things that didn't interest him, and he said to me, 'Do what you think is best'. That said, I believed it. I began to live my life as a young Christian. In time, my oldest sister, my youngest sister and my older brother were all converted.'

However, his parents' lack of interest did not last. First his mother and then his father began to oppose their children's newfound faith-and in particular Rene, who had brought all the trouble into the house. 'It was said to be "Protestant" and therefore in opposition to the family heritage. So we were forbidden to go to church meetings and our Bibles were burned. Then the opposition became more intense and it degenerated into open persecution and spiritual combat. One morning I found my mother putting powder into our morning coffee and I found she had consulted witches-they're called soucières in

Marseille and they advertise widely-in order to put a spell on us so that we would leave our faith.'

As he looks back on it all, Rene can see that becoming a Christian put him at odds with the family's beliefs, prejudices and superstitions. In fact his youngest sister left her faith during this period and it was 20 years before she renewed the commitment she made at that time. But the weight of the truth Rene experienced eventually brought many of his family to a Christian conversion. Even his father became a Christian, just three weeks before his death.

The opposition did not prevent Rene from doing what he believed, however. 'I went to church in spite of being forbidden, knowing there would be a punishment waiting for me at home. I knew that I had to persevere. To stay away would have been very difficult for me. A group of people there became my second family. At home, in my own big family, there was a certain emptiness, which was filled by the family of God.'

At church, Rene became part of the youth group, which was about 15 strong. The youth group leader, with whom Rene developed a deep friendship, was a faithful and encouraging friend during his early years as a Christian. Also very important to him was the pastor of the church through his clear and consistent teaching of the Bible.

Thirty years on, Rene Galbes has a ministry as a Christian psychotherapist. He is involved in counselling and training in churches all over France, travelling into Switzerland and further afield. Married to Damaris, he has four children, in their teens and 20s. For many years, they have lived in the small town of Gignac-La-Nerthe, just out of Marseille in the Provence region. Provence, is an area of great beauty-rugged and weathered white limestone hills scattered with scrub and trees, and valleys full of fertile soil able to support vineyard after vineyard. There are no grazing animals in sight and virtually no fences. The mountain roads give stunning views of a blue, blue Mediterranean Sea nestling into golden sands of picturesque bays.

Rene has been involved in some form of Christian service for more than 25 years. He has been involved in founding churches and pastoring the fellowships coming from that work. He has also used his gifts in itinerant evangelism and Christian counselling.

Rene was only 16 years old when he was first challenged to make a commitment to full-time service. He heard a young French missionary just back from Africa, Yves Perrier, at a missionary meeting. M. Perrier remarked on how few Frenchmen he saw in Christian service in Africa: 'Frenchmen preferred their slippers to their faith.'

In an appeal for consecration that night, Rene responded. 'The Lord spoke to me. It was very clear. He told me to get up. It was very difficult. I was the only boy-there was a girl as well. The pastor and elders then prayed for our consecration to serve the Lord.'

He decided to pursue a profession that would bring him into contact with people globally. He chose nursing, graduating from his training near the top of his class. After his early schooling difficulties, he saw this as both a gift from God, and a responsibility. From the time of his conversion, with its parallel change in his attitude, his scholastic capacities and his studies improved enormously.

He met Damaris during his nursing training. She was a fellow classmate and Christian also seeking an avenue to serve God. Both 21 when they married, they turned their attention to missionary work in Africa. While they were negotiating with a mission serving in Chad, tribal troubles erupted there. The pastor they were to replace was kidnapped by rebels so the mission halted their departure plans. Still thinking of Africa, they enrolled at Lamorly Bible School for a year's study. While there, they were challenged by the spiritual state of their own country, seeing France for the first time as a mission field. At the end of the year they went to L'Aveyron, in south-central France, where they stayed for five years before moving on to itinerant evangelism, then returning to Provence.

Rene and Damaris continue to serve God. Their professional training in psychology and psychiatry has led to Rene's counselling ministry as a Christian psychotherapist. He has also taught in the Institût Biblique du Dauphine at Grenoble in the French Alps.

All this is a long way from the angry young man who failed his entrance tests to panel beating. This may have been part of a plan. It is hard to develop subtle conversations of depth in a panel-beater's workshop!

well, what made the difference?

Rene's family had strong cultural and spiritual beliefs, yet rather than leading him to Christian faith, they produced rebellion. What can we learn from his story?

1. The faith of Rene's family was probably centred more in culture and tradition than the living Christ. Are there times when we tend to accentuate the 'trappings' of our faith rather than the true centre? How can that be a stumbling block to young people? How can we ensure that they will be pointed to what matters?

2. Rene describes some of his disillusionment with his family's beliefs as rebellion, yet it was this rebellion, which led him to a faith of his own. Did he have a reason to rebel? What sort of faith would he have had if he didn't rebel? Is it

possible to present a faith that young people will grow into without rebelling against?

3. The priest who listened to Rene's arguments loaned him a Bible, validated his questioning and searching, yet didn't 'tell him' the gospel. Another pastor explained the meaning of the Bible to Rene. How do we balance the twin needs of guiding a person towards discovering the truth for themselves and unashamedly pointing them to the truth? Are we doing it with the young people closest to us?

seed in good soil

Andrew Ramsbottom

When Andrew Ramsbottom's girl friend first mentioned his name at home, her grandmother said, 'For goodness' sake don't marry a man with a name like Ramsbottom.' She ignored this advice and today Gill Mee is Gill Ramsbottom.

'At least she can't say she wasn't warned,' says Andrew, grinning. 'It's a name that takes a bit of getting used to. For me, taking my name on board was something that happened at a camp, way back when I was nine. They were calling out the names of the kids in the different leaders' groups, and when they said 'Ramsbottom', the whole camp fell about laughing- leaders, campers and all. It was right there that I decided that I was not ashamed of or embarrassed by my surname, that I'd be proud of it. This is a key thing that I remember in my life.'

Camps have been significant in Andrew's life in a number of ways. His close-knit family often went hiking, as a family or with friends. They lived in Uitenhage, 35 kilometres from Port Elizabeth in the Eastern Cape Province of South Africa, just two hours' walk from the country's biggest wilderness area. The family often camped there at Hell's Gate, a spot also popular for youth camps. So Andrew, along with his siblings Duncan and Megan, grew up very much at home in the outdoors.

The family could be described as an upper middle class family with their own car as well as a company car, a full time maid and a fashionable address. Traditionally they spent the Christmas holidays together at Buffalo Bay, a beach resort on the Cape coast, a four and a half hour drive from home along the Garden

Route. Their house was just two sets of steps from the main beach and looked out over the whole bay. During the long summer holidays they spent a lot of time swimming, surfing and snorkelling. Andrew's maternal grandfather, Pop - the actual owner of the house - taught them to fish. His other grandparents were usually present too.

The children were sent regularly to Sunday School for their Christian teaching. They were taught to pray as they went to bed and grace was always part of family meals. But there was no practice of the family reading the Bible together or of family prayer. In the family, Andrew's Pop had the most Christian influence on him and his paternal Nana was also a help. Both spent devotional time with the Bible or with other inspirational booklets and sang in the choir at their church, the old Methodist church in Uitenhage's town centre.

Andrew's parents were married there in 1961 having grown up in Uitenhage. It was an industrial town of some 150,000 people and because of the South African politics of the day, people were required to live in clearly delineated areas-whites lived on one side of the Swartkops River and blacks on the other, with coloureds living in the hills behind.

Uitenhage is a spacious place, its jacaranda trees giving a glorious purple tone in the spring. Summers are dry, without being arid. In a white population that was predominantly Afrikaans, the Ramsbottoms, being English-speaking were part of a minority group. Andrew, the oldest child, was born there in 1965.

As the three children grew, their parents took them to the local suburban Methodist church, dropping the children off at Sunday School in the morning and collecting them later in the day. This became the pattern of Andrew's childhood. During that time he was taught by a variety of Sunday School teachers, now largely forgotten, who made Sunday School an enjoyable place to be and taught him from the Bible. 'I really enjoyed Sunday School,' he said. 'I enjoyed what I learned there.' His parents encouraged that learning, even though they attended church irregularly and did not practice formal Christian devotions at home. Yet the principles of family living they instilled in the children provided responsive ground for later teaching from other quarters.

Andrew was ten and a half when he first went to a Scripture Union summer 'mini' camp geared for primary school-aged children and held at a Dutch Reformed campsite just out of Uitenhage. The one hundred campers were drawn from the wider Uitenhage-Port Elizabeth area. The campsite is set among trees in a large grassed area with natural artesian springs that provide the town with water.

'My group leader made a real impression on me,' Andrew said. 'He came from Port Elizabeth and was a real fun guy to be with - you felt like someone special, being in his group. He was the sort of guy who was into everything, and he made you want to get into it too. And you could tell, when he and the other leaders talked about their faith, that it was real to them. They were into that too.

'We spent time in the swimming pool each morning - it was quite deep, and allowed for plenty of diving and bombing and all that sort of thing. There were bush walks and scavenger hunts, and each morning there was a quiet time - time spent with the Bible, on a guided basis. There were also morning 'marquee times', called 'marquee times' because at some stage in the camp's history they'd actually put up a marquee to hold them in. By the time I got there, they were being held in the meeting hall, but the name had stuck. After lunch, there was a thirty minute break, a sort of siesta, and during the break you could go to Keenites. It was at Keenites that I made my response to Jesus, to become a Christian.

'Keenites was for people who were keen. It was a voluntary time. Everyone had to be quiet, and you could choose to be quiet on your own or, if you were keen to ask any Christian questions or talk with the leaders or something, you could go to Keenites. You couldn't go swimming or anything noisy or group based. It was a time for re-gathering. When I look at it now, I can see it was a time when the leaders could free kids up to go to Keenites, when they wouldn't be missing out on anything else.

I'd been doing some thinking at the meetings, the marquee times. I'd had all this Sunday school teaching through the years, so the background was there. Then when those leaders I respected made it look real, and the marquee meetings started spelling out the challenges, I started to think seriously. I wanted to ask more, so I went along to Keenites.

'I talked to the camp dad-Fred Delport was his name. He was a bit older than the camp leaders and it was his job to add some mature wisdom to the general enthusiasm of the team. We sat under the pines and he chatted with me about what it means to be a Christian. We went through a booklet and we talked about the cost of it, how I would have to stand up at school, and when I prayed a prayer of commitment with him it was well meant. I asked for forgiveness for my sin, and for Jesus to become my Saviour and friend, and I knew I'd become a Christian. It was a 10 year old's response, but I knew what I was doing, and I knew what the cost was, and I was quite happy to do it. Later on in the camp, I remember we sang, 'I have decided to follow Jesus-the cross before me, the world behind me, no turning back'-and I sang it quite deliberately. It had a new meaning for me. I had become a Christian.'

So a young man's Christian journey had begun. Where did it take him in the immediate future and in the longer term?

'Well, in the immediate future, I went home and announced it to my family, as Fred Delport had suggested. They weren't completely enthusiastic-kind of looked at me with a "yeah, yeah, so what?" look. After all, they'd sent me along to the camp, and often taken me to church. They'd have said I was a Christian already-what's this new deal? But I knew. I'd made a decision and a commitment to live by, and things were not the same.

I had a commitment to read the Bible too. I was keen to do this, because I knew it was the source of the things I had been learning about. So I went home with some Bible reading notes I'd been given at the Scripture Union camp, and I read the Bible with the aid of these notes, with real interest for the first week or so. But then the drive wavered a bit, and all the other things the holidays offered crowded out the hours, and the Bible reading slowly waned, until I went back to school and I'd virtually come to a standstill. That's when I met another significant adult. She was the teacher who took the voluntary Scripture Union group in the school.

I hadn't gone to the Christian group in the past. But at the camp, they had encouraged us to go to our school groups when we got back. I was keen to do the right things, and to grow in my faith, so I went, and I met Miss Preller. She asked us about the holidays and what we'd been doing, and one thing led to another, till I told her I'd become a Christian at the camp I was on. She was encouraging about it, and took to asking me from time to time how I was getting on with reading my Bible. She wasn't dramatic about it-what she was doing wasn't vastly out of the way-but it helped me a lot. It was a great encouragement to have someone show that they understood, and cared enough to ask. The Christian group was important to me. It used to meet once a week during school break for a twenty minute prayer meeting, and once a week for an hour after school, when there would be singing, memory verses learned and tested, Bible reading, prayer time with Miss Preller-a kind of group quiet time.

I enjoyed that but I also had some moments at school when I had to learn what it was to be a Christian when not everyone around was helpful. Muir College was a boys' school with a strong tradition, one of the oldest schools in South Africa. My father and grandfather were both old boys, and it had a strong Old Boys' association. There were 350 boys in the primary school. The Scripture Union group had maybe 20 core members, and life in the school at large could get a bit rough, in terms of bad language and off coloured jokes and some bullying here and there. You had to know what you were prepared to stand for. In that first year Miss Preller was really important in holding the group together and providing personal encouragement. She used to plan the program as well as run it, in addition to her ordinary teaching duties.'

The next few years followed a predictable enough pattern. There were some periods of special Christian enthusiasm and some of neglect and all the ordinary pursuits of developing boyhood. There continued to be the family holidays at Buffalo Bay, full of surf, swimming and sand skiing on the large sand dunes with boards touched up with floor polish. At twelve, Andrew did a sailing course and there was snorkelling too. Andrew and his brother Duncan used to dive to retrieve lead sinkers lost by the local fishermen and then sell them back to them. His Pop taught him to fish, when he was able to bring him in from playing in the dunes. Pop was also a valuable Christian influence in those years, initiating Christian conversation sometimes, but more often just being there. He was a good influence-calming the brothers down, for example, in their not-infrequent scraps. Altogether, it was a wholesome and healthy period.

Andrew, with Duncan and Megan, continued to attend Sunday

school through the final years at primary school. Around a hundred and twenty young people were involved, ranging in age from under five to fourteen. All were from a similar social background-English-speaking, upper middle class, white, and drawn from the two English-speaking schools in Uitenhage, the boys' and girls' schools.

As he moved on toward High School at Muir College, Andrew's involvement at his church grew. He helped run the Scripture Union program at school and the youth program at church and became a keen core member of the high school Student Christian Association. This voluntary Christian group met in their own time under the guidance of a staff member and a number of senior boys. 'And how important those boys were,' says Andrew now. 'There were only about 30 boys in the group, but the head boy was its chairman. There were various other school heroes. I really looked up to them, and they were a terrific encouragement to us young, new Christians. I felt really proud to be part of that group. We met each week, with various speakers or for other studies and activities, and sometimes there was a joint camp with the girls' school.

'Occasionally there was a week-long mission in the school. We'd get someone in from Youth for Christ or the local churches or wherever. There would be lunchtime or evening concerts and other things in the school breaks and after school. We took RE lessons too-Religious Education. Some of the non-Christian teachers who had to teach RE were quite happy for some Christian to come in and take it on their behalf.

'The SCA group was very active and a valuable part of the High School. It became important to me in my Christian development. When I was 16, one of its missions was taken by the African Enterprise organisation. There I made a teenaged response to God to follow on from my childhood conversion. My childhood experience had been real and I had no doubt about it. But at one of the evening meetings of the African Enterprise mission taken by Rev. Bill Winter, I got a whole new vision of what it all really meant, and I knew I had to do something about it. There was no time to talk to anyone at the meeting because I was already late and had to go home but at the next school meeting I responded to the general invitation to talk to team members of the mission at school break time or after school. A list with available time slots was put up on a notice board and you marked down when you could make it to go along. I sneaked in to do this when no one was looking, and I spent time talking to one of the team members that afternoon. It was a personal and private time with just me and the counsellor and God. I realised something more of what full commitment was about and knelt down there and then in that school classroom, and prayed a prayer of renewed commitment.

'I was just going out through the door when I ran into a friend coming in, my Scout patrol leader. He was 18, a couple of years older than me and in the final year at school.

"What are you doing here?" he asked, and I had to tell him. "What about you?" I said, and he replied, "Same thing. Would you stay with me?" So I knelt there with him as he told God of his commitment.

'Looking back on it, the African Enterprise meetings contained a mix of good features. They came to both the boys' and girls' schools for the mission events. Evening meetings were held at our church, which had a good hall and an active youth group. The meetings had a blend of music and drama and drew between a hundred and twenty and a hundred and fifty kids. The keynote speaker gave a clear challenge about Christian commitment, which prompted me. In terms of culture and language they were a mixed team. This meant they could only get access to the English schools, because the mixed nature of the team kept them out of the Afrikaans schools.

'One thing led to another, of course. My greater leadership with the youth group got me into other related activities, and then one day I got dragged along to help with a Scripture Union children's camp. I didn't want to go-a friend took me-and I realised there that God had a ministry for me in children's work.'

That ministry was to develop over the next few years. When he finished school, Andrew went on to Rhodes University at Grahamstown on the edge of the Little Karroo, an hour's drive from Uitenhage. Last century, Grahamstown was in the centre of the 1820 British settler movement but today it is a dedicated university town. Rhodes University, with 3000 students, is one of the smallest universities in South Africa. Sixty per cent of students live on campus, which takes up half the town's land, the rest consisting of town and schools. The town's heritage is English and each June it holds an English festival during the holiday period. There is a population of 80,000, 10,000 of whom are English, and the town boasts 52 churches. No wonder Grahamstown is known as the 'city of saints'! Many of its various private and government schools are boarding schools.

It proved to be a valuable, formative time for Andrew, giving him much scope to develop as a Christian. He joined the Student Christian Association, the Methodist Society, worshipped at a Baptist church, helped run a Presbyterian youth group, and took part in various Scripture Union children's holiday programs as well as a Scripture Union mission at a private school. Informal contacts with Christian peers, such as prayer groups and one-off mission groups, encouraged his faith.

It was here that he met Gill Mee. Both had been on a Scripture Union school leavers' camp at the end of Gill's final year of school and they got on well. Gill often saved a seat for him at lectures as she was keen on his friend who she thought might turn up with him. During the process they became at ease with each other, but it took them until well into their university courses to work out the obvious. Today she is Gill Ramsbottom.

Andrew is now in his early thirties. He and Gill have lived in Auckland, New Zealand, since 1995 where Andrew still follows Jesus as a full time children's worker for Scripture Union. Significantly he finds the work challenging and rewarding, believing that this is what God wants him to be doing for now.

His parents moved to Port Elizabeth some years ago when his father's company in Uitenhage closed. They are now regular churchgoers and buy for themselves the Bible reading notes their son once organised for them. Megan is thinking of doing missionary work while Duncan is an electrical engineer who gives some time to Scripture Union activities in the Cape Town area.

Andrew continues to develop through taking his turn at leading his small group at his church and in helping others. He is growing too through taking the Bible College of New Zealand's Mission Internship course where Scripture and Christian history have come alive for him.

well, what made the difference?

Andrew Ramsbottom has benefited from Christian teaching and from family stability and care, which have given him opportunities to flourish as a person. Let's think about some of these in more detail.

1. His Sunday School days provided enjoyable experiences and knowledge that were to be the seedbed for more specific, Christian challenges to take root later in life. What sorts of experiences can later provide valuable background for adolescents? What knowledge is important? What does this say about the content of our programs for children?

2. Godly grandparents undoubtedly prayed for him. Can you think of ways of providing strong prayer backing for young people who may not have it? How can you encourage those who are already praying?

3. Pivotal experiences at camps provided Andrew with attractive role models and deliberate Christian teaching and challenge. How can we ensure that these sorts of advantages are available to the children and young people with whom we work?

4. Miss Preller encouraged Andrew's faith, specifically in the area of prayer and Bible use. How important was this? Are we assisting our young people in these ways?

5. Andrew's experience of school missions gave fresh opportunities for personal challenge. What on-going faith challenges are available to 'sharpen' our young people? In what ways can we provide these opportunities?

he went for the perks

Wayne Dixon

As a staunch supporter of London's Arsenal football club,
Wayne Dixon understood the sacrifices needed to follow the
football: queues, long train trips for away games, goalless
draws in the pouring rain. He understood also that to play
football required certain sacrifices. But he never anticipated
that one sacrifice would be attending a Bible Club run by the
London City Mission.

The London City Mission is an inter-denominational
organisation that has shared the gospel with the people of
London for over a hundred and sixty years. In the early 1970s
the Mission ran a Gospel Hall in the East End suburb of
Leytonstone. A Bible Club was held there on Sunday afternoons
under the umbrella of an inter-denominational organisation
called the Covenanters. This organisation has existed for some
60-70 years, running every type of youth activity.

In Leytonstone in the early 1970s, they ran the Bible Club as
well as club night on a weeknight. On the club night, younger
people from the community could go along and play table
tennis, badminton or maybe basketball. Then a football team
was put together, playing weekend matches against other youth
groups or club sides. These opportunities were particularly
attractive to young people who were sick of hanging around the
shops or the local housing estates.

Wayne became aware of the Covenanters' group through his
older brothers who were keen on the games and enjoyed the
club nights. He learnt quickly amid the rough-and-tumble

backyard and street games in which little brothers always get knocked around. He became skilled at manoeuvring a ball past a bunch of older brothers and their mates. And he was old enough to attend the club nights.

However, there was a catch. Unless boys were bona fide attenders at the Bible Club on Sunday afternoon, the Covenanters refused to pick them in their Saturday afternoon football team. Some of the locals found this too big a price to pay and gave the whole thing away. But Wayne, knowing there was no such thing as a free lunch, considered it a fair bargain. So by coming on a Sunday afternoon, he guaranteed his availability for football on Saturday and club nights on weekdays. His family was not part of any church so it didn't clash with anything else he did.

Wayne's parents were originally from Jamaica. They moved to England in the late 1950s, part of the waves of migration of those years. Three of their eight children still lived with relatives in the West Indies. Wayne, the second youngest, was the third member of the family to be born in London. The East End of London is a very mixed area, in both racial and ethnic terms. The family had no pretensions, and like many of the East End residents, they took an oblique view of anyone who in their opinion did have. Wayne's mother worked at a local hospital, in the domestic area. His father had a number of jobs at different times-building, general labouring and bits and pieces here and there. He was a part time reggae musician, playing the trumpet and singing at occasional gigs.

However, with seven family members in London, there was not always a lot of money to spare, and they learned to make the best of what they had. Hardship sorts out certain qualities in people. So Wayne understood the approach: 'You want to play in our football team, you earn the membership dues. We'll see you on Sunday.'

So he went on Sunday, with mixed motives. 'I had my first introduction to the gospel there. What was I-eight or nine? We used to go along and have some teaching and a quiz based on the last week's lesson, and a talk by a leader.' Wayne's agile mind rehearsed and stored each week's memory verse, such as John 3:16, Psalm 37:4, Proverbs 3:5. 'It was all rote stuff, just like learning your times tables or your address when you were very little. But it was all going in and it stayed.'

Of course times tables, though very helpful, are in the end just numbers. Wayne was storing a message that has changed whole cultures and the course of history. 'God loved the world so much that he gave his Son so that all who believe may have everlasting life.' ... 'Delight yourself in the Lord and he will give you the desires of your heart.' ... 'Trust in the Lord and acknowledge him and he will make your paths straight.' As Wayne recalls, 'I wasn't really interested in the Bible part but I got my first introduction to the gospel, which I wasn't getting from any other place. And I got to play in the football team.'

He liked the club activities too. Now in his 30s, he still enjoys table tennis and badminton, both introduced to him at the club. And of course, he's still an Arsenal supporter.

While Wayne was simply 'doing time' in the Bible Club, he remembers seeing something special in the teachers. He recalls that they were faithful in their commitment, clear in their vision and sincere in their beliefs. Wayne still speaks of them with gratitude. 'Two of them I still have contact with-Robert Emblem and Jim Wyper, who worked for the London City Mission. Jim was employed by the mission; Robert was a volunteer who earned his living as a banker.

'They were instrumental in my understanding of Christianity. To them, it wasn't a job or a hobby. It was their life. They got alongside us and they invested hours in us, and gave us a grounding in the word. A friend, by the name of Chris, became a Christian around that time. Today, he's a Baptist minister in South London-another reward for encouragement and time. Those men gave prayer and resources and themselves to a group of very mixed interest. Half of us were only there to play the games.'

Although he may not have gone along out of any desire to hear the gospel, he did get to learn a lot about Jesus. The regular Sunday teaching focused on the four gospels. From the age of about eight, Wayne knew quite a bit about the life of Jesus-what Jesus did, what he said, the places he went to and the people he met. The message of Jesus hadn't struck home but he could give a good account of much of the material surrounding his life. What is more, he noticed a similarity in the lives of his teachers and some of those followers of Jesus in the gospels.

But the gospel for Wayne was like the advice of a football coach to a young player: as one perspective or bit of advice was acknowledged, the whole game plan started to take shape. Wayne was starting to realise he couldn't go through life making up the rules as he went. And those texts of timeless wisdom he had been memorising were all there somewhere in his head.

One evening things crystallised for him in an ordinary but profound way. 'We had a special service in our hall on New Year's Eve, in 1976,' Wayne recalls. 'They called it a Watchnight Service. There was an evening of fun, fellowship and food. There was a film, too. Then there was a service, to see the New Year in. I can't remember the details of the talk but I do remember the speaker getting to the point and phrasing his key question for the night-"How about starting the New Year on God's side?" And I thought, "Well, why not? I know a little about Jesus." '

Wayne understood that Jesus came to earth, was crucified and that he rose from the dead. 'I knew that he was a good man and a good teacher. I knew that he cared for people and I knew a lot about his teaching. But until then, it was all history and knowledge. None of it was personal. But here was this speaker saying 'What about being on God's side?' and I decided right then, that I wanted to. If Jesus did all this for me, then I wanted my life to count for him. If I could know that he loved me and was willing to forgive me, then I wanted to follow him. So in my own way, aged 11, I decided that night while the speaker was finishing his remarks, that that's what I wanted to do.'

Wayne doesn't remember any call to make a public commitment but he does remember making a decision deep within in his heart. 'I never said anything to anyone. I just decided, within myself, what I wanted to do in response to the challenge I had been given. When I look back, I can see it must have been a good time for me to do that. It was only months later that I had the biggest difficulty of my life. My parents split up.'

His parents' separation devastated him. Wayne loved them both very much. 'I was appalled that our family, which I held so dear, was to be shattered. If I hadn't made a decision to join God's side back at the New Year, I certainly wouldn't have done it in March. As it was, I was terribly angry with God for allowing it to happen. You'd have thought he could have stopped it. If he was so big, so strong and so mighty, and if there was nothing he couldn't do (as one of our songs said), why couldn't he have prevented this break-up from happening? You wouldn't think a thing like that would be too much of a challenge to someone like him. Yet here he was, doing nothing, while my life was falling down around my ears. I felt sadly let down and I blamed God. It wouldn't have been a good time for anyone to try to get me to follow God just then.'

While it seemed to Wayne that God couldn't have cared less that his parents' marriage fell to pieces, his friends at Covenanters were the exact opposite. They didn't try to take away the pain but rather, listened to him. 'Most of them knew my family or they knew the situation and something of the problems, and they were wise enough not to lecture me when I was complaining about God. They gave me time and room to move, and they listened to me. As I found them patient and sympathetic and caring, I felt accepted and loved, and my anger turned to understanding. I especially remember Robert Emblem being there for me. He was in his mid-20s, I suppose, and he just gave me space. We're still in touch today.'

When a marriage falls apart, only the foolish think there is some simple lesson to be learned or advice to give which will dissolve the pain. Wayne's friends at the Covenanters were wise enough to know this and, rather than compound the pain, they demonstrated the truth of God's presence for him in a way that no amount of theological talk could have begun to do.

At an early age he became aware of something that, he says, 'some people have to wait years for. Christians are not immunised against life's sufferings and trials. God does not intervene across my parents' wishes just to make life easier for me. But he is present in the middle of it, and he has his representatives among the processes of it. Paul lists all the trials in Romans 8 and then says, "In all these things, we are more than conquerors." He didn't say, "From all these things." I learned this early, and it's been a prominent teaching point through the years. Still, when I'm chatting to people about Jesus, I try to remember how important it was for me when I was suffering, for other people to understand it. One of my memory verses came from Hebrews 13–"I will never leave you or forsake you" (verse 5). If life is not freed from problems, Jesus is nevertheless there among the problems. That's been my experience now for over 20 years. As a matter of fact, we had a Covenanters theme song that reflects a similar sort of thing–"Be strong and courageous," it said, based on Joshua 1. You don't have to be either strong or courageous if there aren't any trials.'

As he was struggling to make sense of the pain, three years of memory verses and Bible history, stored away mechanically, were starting to come to very good use. 'This teaching was beginning to come alive to me. There were a whole lot of people whose stories I knew and who clearly had their problems, too. What about Saul? Or Job? What about Jesus himself? They didn't desire what they got either. The Bible was proving itself to me as a book whose people knew life, just as I was learning about life. My decision to follow God might have been quiet, and it was certainly recent, but it was already facing a trial and proving, with the help of others, to be powerfully relevant. Being a Christian is the most important decision I have ever made and I am grateful for it.'

Wayne's wrestle with God following his parents' separation was a tussle known only to himself. In fact, it wasn't till seven months later that he made any sort of public acknowledgment of his decision to follow Jesus. 'I didn't tell anyone at the time that I had made such a decision. It was a quiet thing during the meeting on New Year's Eve and it was followed by all the family trauma, and I just never said anything to anybody. It wasn't until later that I made any kind of comment.

'We were on this camp. It was down at Littlehampton, in Sussex-south of England-and the Covenanters were running a boys' adventure camp, a chance for some of the local kids to go away for a week of games, outings and teaching sessions. I went with some others from Leytonstone. One of the leaders said, early in the camp, that any of the boys who were Christians who would like to come along, were welcome to meet at a given time and place after the evening meal, for encouragement.

That's exactly what I did-to the great surprise of the leaders from my own group, who didn't know that I saw myself as a Christian and who didn't know themselves quite how they saw me. They were really pleased. I told them about my New Year's Eve decision and they were genuinely encouraged. They hadn't known about this particular piece of fruit from their labours and I was an example of one of the works of God that comes as a surprise even to those involved in it. This was my first experience of beginning to go public about my faith. I was glad that they were pleased. Later, I came to consider it had been a mistake not to tell anyone, after I learned to appreciate the encouragement that people give to you.'

During high school, Wayne was quite shy about his faith. He was 16 or 17, in the 6th form at Tom Hood Senior High School in London's East End, before he made any kind of public statement of faith. 'It came about when two or three other boys and I thought it would be good to start a Christian group in the school. We got permission from the head of the 6th form-and then we had to announce it to the school in general.'

Wayne found it 'really tough' to stand publicly in front of a large group of his peers at a high school. 'But,' he says, 'we did it! We got the group going, and ran it for the next two years. I can't say it took the school by storm-it was always small, with about five or six attenders but it met regularly for prayer, encouragement and teaching, and it was significant for me at that time.'

It was 1983 and Wayne's last year at school when the path he would take as a Christian became clearer. It was at Spring Harvest, a Christian festival held every Easter with speakers, seminars and workshops of every description. The festival is held at two or three different venues. Organisers hire a holiday camp in a town, advertise the event widely and use the resort's facilities. One might attend a seminar on Holy Spirit deliverance at the Roxy Theatre or a discipleship course in the Moonraker Nightclub. They are big events, with attendances totalling around 70,000 and contributors coming from anywhere in the world.

Wayne attended the event at Prestatyn, in Wales, with a group from his Gospel Hall in Leytonstone. 'We went for a week and a volunteer from the London City Mission came along to help us find our way around. I think her name was Tania. I didn't know her very well, hardly at all. Anyway, at some point in the week, she gave me a real challenge when she said to me that I needed to be a bit more serious about my commitment to God. If I remember, I think she may have used the term 'passenger Christian'. I was pretty upset about it, actually-that someone I didn't really know should challenge me in so direct a way. But as a consequence of her challenge, I really did begin to see a need for change.

'When I got home from the camp, I went to see the minister at a local Baptist church, to ask him if I could be baptised. I knew about baptism but I'd put it off for some years. If anyone had asked me, I'd have to have said that I didn't really see it as necessary. After Spring Harvest, though, I felt that I wanted to do it. I wanted to stand up, be seen and do what I knew Jesus had left instructions for us to do. I felt that God was asking me and I was showing obedience. When I look back, I'm grateful for the challenge that I didn't really appreciate at the time. I was 18 when I was baptised at the Central Baptist Church in Walthamstow, in East London. I went there because that was where Robert Emblem was a member. Baptism was a very special moment for me, significant.'

The year was also significant for Wayne in a couple of other ways. At Spring Harvest he picked up a brochure from Scripture Union. They were advertising their year's program of residential holidays and he applied to help as a leader on a holiday for 11-

14 year olds. 'I filled in the forms and got my references together,' Wayne remembers. 'And then I found that they also ran a sports holiday. This was right up my street, since sports have always been a major love. I thought Scripture Union might just transfer my references from the other holiday camp to the sports one. But it turned out that at 18 I was a bit young for what they needed on the sports holiday. I'd just left school but I ended up going to it anyway, as one of the campers. I was able to be a leader the following year. I'm still involved. On that holiday we saw lives changed. It was one of the highlights of the year.'

The other major event in 1983 for Wayne was that he left school that year and moved to Slough, to do a two year college course in Business Studies. 'It wasn't my first choice-I actually wanted to train as a teacher but I failed to get the necessary exam results to be accepted for teacher training. It was disappointing to me, because I'd always wanted to be a teacher-or a professional footballer! But it wasn't to be. So I did the Business Studies course at Slough, after praying and talking with Christian friends. It was another object lesson to me that a blocked-off ambition is not the same as the end of the world. It just meant that I got to follow a different direction. I worked for three years with the Seiko Watch Company, as an after-sales man, when I'd finished my Business course.'

Wayne is still in Slough but no longer with Seiko. Since 1988, he has found himself working with young people in and around schools after all, not as a teacher but with Scripture Union. Slough, in the county of Berkshire, is about 20 km west of London. Its population of 100,000 includes many races, nationalities and ethnic groups, all reflected in the schools he visits for Scripture Union. The three towns he covers are concentrated within a radius of about 15 km, but their population is made up of a varied cross-section of people.

As a 'schools worker', Wayne links up with local secondary schools. He loves his job. As well as Slough, his round also includes Maidenhead and Windsor, where the royal castle is. He speaks at assemblies, lunchtime group meetings, in Religious Education classes or just hangs around with pupils in their free times at lunch times and in breaks. He is known to school authorities and liases officially with them, never attempting to infiltrate schools in an underhand way. He has many chances to get to know the pupils informally as well and to talk to them about Jesus. He finds the kids welcoming, both at the schools and outside, and many wander up to him in the town and talk about anything. He is absolutely clear that God has called him into his work, which arose from a variety of informal opportunities where he spoke with young people. He relishes the chances he has to meet so many young people, getting to know some of them well and explaining Jesus to many who have no church contact. He has found it easy to invite interested young friends to the Scripture Union network of camps and holidays, and has remained especially fond of the sports camp he has attended over the years.

Tom Giles first invited him to this camp. This Scripture Union leader has influenced him greatly. Wayne first attended four camps as a volunteer leader and since then, camp has been part of his job. Some job! The camp is held at Basingstoke in Hampshire, not too far away to the southwest. Campers are offered a variety of sports-football, badminton, cricket, table tennis, archery, swimming, tennis, golf, squash, trampolining, rugby among them. Although campers are mostly from England, they come from all over the UK, and some are from Germany, Italy and France. It is little wonder that Wayne Dixon, the sports-loving kid from the East End, not too far from the Old Kent Road, regards it as the highlight of the year.

Right now, Wayne is settled in Slough. He is still a member at the Baptist church he first attended when he arrived as a student.

Its members have cared for him in countless ways. In his early years there he assisted in their youth events. They supported him and other leaders of a college Christian Union during his Business Studies course. They helped confirm his call into Scripture Union in 1988 and now provide him with his primary Christian support base. Most of his family chose not to pursue the faith actively but look back on their time at the Leytonstone mission positively. Wayne says he is grateful they accept and are tolerant of his stance but he relies on his church for the spiritual connection that only comes from other Christians.

Wayne met his wife at Slough Baptist. Joyce is a nursery nurse- she provides a school-based pre-school education for four-year-olds. They were married in June 1994. His office is at the church and he appreciates the insight and friendship of the pastoral team there. The minister, Rev. Keith Moyes, has been an inspiration to him since he first went to the church as a student. More recently, Rev. Jim Sewell, also on the pastoral team, has been a friend to confide in and a true source of encouragement.

Wayne needs those people. Like everyone, his spiritual journey has its ups and downs, but he is convinced that regularly focusing on Bible reading and prayer, connecting deeply with other Christians and sharing the faith that has changed his life brings lasting joy. He is aware of the promises of God, that they are reliable through the good times and the bad, and that the presence of God's Spirit is closer than that of any other person.

In many ways his development is like that of any young man growing up in Leytonstone, attending the Bible Club so he could play in the football team. He still likes sports, plays table tennis, gets to Highbury to see Arsenal play less often than he'd like to and enjoys music. But Andrew is also different. He found faith. He also has the desire that young people will be put in touch with God, just as those before him put him in touch with God. God has produced a pattern out of the pieces of his life that, if he had kept making up his own rules, would be even more scattered now than when he first attended the Covenanters back when he was eight.

well, what made the difference?

Wayne Dixon's journey to faith raises interesting questions about the way young people become Christians.

1. The local youth club tapped into Wayne's keenest passion, football, and he was happy enough to participate knowing there were 'strings attached'. What tensions do you see between having 'up front' motives over the purpose of an activity such as this and being more subtle?

2. Wayne experienced the best of Christian friendship after his parents separated. No one tried to find some plan of God amid the pain or make him forget the hurt and put on a 'brave Christian face'. What mistakes do Christians often make when someone is in pain? What can be a more effective response?

3. The challenge to Wayne by the Spring Harvest camp leader to deepen his faith was confronting but effective. Who do you know who might benefit from a direct question or comment about their faith as you see it lived out? Is there a challenge to accept for yourself first?

still asking the questions
Tarsh Koia

Natasha Celia Marama Koia curiously owes her first significant Christian experience to the Jehovah's Witnesses. When she was about 10 or 11, 'Tarsh' first began religious education classes at Waikirikiri School, in Gisborne, on the east coast of New Zealand's North Island. She noticed one of her friends always left the classroom before these classes began and Tarsh became curious and asked her why. 'I'm a Jehovah's Witness,' Tarsh remembers her saying, 'We don't believe what they believe.'

The whole concept of believing or not believing such things was quite strange to Tarsh. She recalls that one day, her friend asked if she would like to come along to a Bible study her mother held. 'I was interested, so I went along. Also, I thought I'd be able to go out of class like her-and that'd be cool. I'd be a Jehovah's Witness and it'd be different.'

But when she went once to her friend's Bible study, she felt very uneasy. 'It was like something in me was saying, "This is not right". I went once and never went back. I had no inner peace-there was something freaky inside. I was only ten and I'd never had any Christian teaching, but it was very real. So I told my friend, I wouldn't go back. But when I went back to religious education class, I was really interested and something inside of me said, "This is the truth". I think I accepted Jesus about then. I certainly knew God was there.'

Tarsh's story really begins years earlier. She was born in Gisborne in March of 1973. And when asked about her conversion, she hesitates. 'It's a long story. It's a process really. I'm a Maori and it's not an individual thing. It's all tied up in the whanau.'

The 'whanau' is the Maori concept of family and is not confined to Mum, Dad and 2.3 children. The whanau is large, fluid and difficult to pin down. It is made up of the parents, their parents, the children and the grandchildren, or mokopuna, as well as all the relations-the aunts and uncles and cousins and in-laws. It breathes identity into everything and everyone within its compass. If you talk to a Maori of anything significant in life, you come across the reality of the whanau.

Tarsh's mother was 21 and unmarried when Tarsh was born. She had gone to Christchurch on a scholarship to go to high school, staying at a Maori girls' hostel. She was a bright girl, the oldest of 11 children and her parents had high hopes for her. They were sure she could be successful-although they weren't clear in what particular field-and that this would benefit the other members of the family. Then she met Tarsh's father and lost her way for a time.

Her parents were very disappointed about the pregnancy, but when she rang them from Christchurch to ask if they would look after the child, they were very pleased. The mother could not care for the baby but she was their mokopuna, and they would. This was whanau. So Tarsh's mother headed north for the birth and Tarsh became her grandparents' youngest charge. She was just a year younger than their last child, her uncle Chris, and they were brought up together. They lived on Huanui Station, then a large dairy and sheep farm, some 70 kilometres north of Gisborne, inland from Tolaga Bay.

Tarsh's grandparents were hardworking New Zealanders. Her grandfather was 50, her grandmother 46. They came from Tikitiki and Ruatoria, about two hours' drive away further up the coast. They met on a sheep farm when he was a shearer and she was a 'fleece-o', someone who handles the fleeces in a shearing shed. They worked hard and played hard. One of the ways to wind down after work was drinking and binge partying. These are some of Tarsh's earliest childhood memories. The children also grew up watching alcohol-induced physical abuse.

Although the family mellowed as the years passed, there were still times of hard drinking. When Tarsh was about nine years old, her grandmother decided she had had enough. One night she packed up the younger children, heading off to Ruatoria to stay with relations on the marae-the traditional Maori gathering place. They were there for six months and Tarsh found it 'so boring'. The marae was 20 minutes out of Ruatoria, with a rural school called Hiru-harama and everything was small.

Looking back with the benefit of hindsight, Tarsh is glad to have been there. 'It was, actually, a great privilege,' as she describes it now. 'Marae living, Maori language, Maori exposure-that's who I am and that's what that place was. It was an expression of the things that have made me.'

She grew up with a natural exposure to the Maori language. 'I learned it, even though I was not taught it. My grandparents spoke Maori a lot, especially on the Coast before they went down to Gisborne. We used it among the whanau.'

Her grandmother went back to the farm and just a short time later, her grandfather retired on doctor's advice and moved to Gisborne. After 22 years on the farm, he now suffered from asthma and bronchitis.

The town of Gisborne was scary, Tarsh recalls. 'It was so big-probably about 35,000 people at the time-and there was a new school and everything.' The school, Waikirikiri School, was predominantly Maori. Gisborne itself has a high proportion of Maori people. To a ten year old girl from outside of Tolaga Bay it was all new, and it was the big world.

'I hadn't had any Christian teaching in those early years,' Tarsh reflected, 'but I've always known God has been with me. It's nothing I'd done, nor that anyone else had done–or, not to me. I believe now it was my grandmother's prayers.'

The couple of years after her experience of the Jehovah's Witnesses saw Tarsh becoming aware of how she fitted in to the broader society, and working out for herself how she was going to react to it. 'We lived in Kaiti. That's the poorer area of Gisborne. It's mostly Maori and we were not rich. We lived off my grandad's superannuation benefit. I remember when I was going to go to High School we didn't have enough money to buy the uniform. We had to wait for the Social Welfare cheque and three days before school started, it still hadn't come. I was dreading having to go to school with no uniform and having kids think we were too poor to afford it. I prayed about it and got a pad and envelope, because I was going to write to Social Welfare and tell them how unjust it all was. I must have been a little activist.'

In fact, the cheque did come in time, and the uniform was available. 'I was very chuffed,' Tarsh remembers, 'and I gave thanks to God.' But her prayers were not usually to do with material things. 'I wanted us to be happy. My grandparents used to fight sometimes, usually to do with drink, and I was scared by it. I used to pray that we would be delivered from the drink. And sometimes I wondered why I couldn't stay with my parents– they were both bright, and surely they should have heaps of money? But they didn't.'

During Tarsh's second year at high school, her mother and little brother moved to Gisborne and spent some time with various aunts and uncles in the area. Tarsh stayed with her mother and brother for a year and during that time her mother became a Christian through a sister of Tarsh's grandmother. She joined a local New Life church fellowship and took Tarsh and her brother along. It was at this time that Tarsh's Christian growth began to bloom.

'It was cool–I loved it all,' she says. 'I had a couple of times when I found myself stopping fights at school and there were also some unfortunate children I wanted to be friendly with. There was one girl who always had bare feet and had to use a school hockey stick to play with, and everyone left her to herself. I used to talk to her. One day a friend said to me, "Tarsha, you just don't talk to people like that." I said, "I can talk to anyone I like. It's not fair for people to tease her." God had given me a mind of my own and I didn't like meanness. And this teaching about Jesus all just seemed to add up.'

But as time passed, the church itself lost its attraction and her mother had to force her and her brother to go. When her mother left for Wellington a year later, Tarsh gave up going. She had liked it, but it had not become hers.

For the next three years she had no church. Then during her fifth year at Gisborne High School, her grandparents became Christians. 'It was a combination of things. Some of my aunts and uncles had become Christians because of my mother. It was a sort of family thing God brought a new hope and a new light into lives that had been quite bad, really–a lot of poverty and sadness. Jesus was real, not just a traditional belief, because he brought a hope from despair and a way out from all the drink and everything.

'Then my grandfather got some spots on his lungs and they were frightened it could be cancer. He was a hard man and unsympathetic to Christianity. But my aunts and uncles prayed for him a lot. Then one day he had his X-ray and the spots were all gone! He was very touched by this. He became a Christian because of it and his wife followed him. She was hardworking woman. She had suffered a lot and she loved her husband. She would have had God earlier, on her own, so when he came to faith, she came too.'

The following year Tarsh made a deliberate decision to go back to church and she joined a youth group. Whether it was a positive experience is open to question. 'It wasn't a Bible teaching youth group at all, more of a "good times together" situation. Some of the kids were vague about the right sort of good times and some of them were sleeping around with each other. I remember thinking, "You guys have lost the plot". Even with my limited background, I knew about that. But I stayed friendly with them. This church was my place for Christian friends.

'I didn't have any Christian friends at school. There were some good kids there, because I was in a good class. But we knew how to work the system and we used to take the odd afternoon off school. There was some partying and drinking too, and plenty of chances to do drugs and sex. But I never did. In many ways, I guess I was the 'good girl' at both youth group and school, and it was because, deep down, that's what I wanted to be. And I didn't mind showing on the surface what I really wanted deep down. I had a lot of freedom-my grandparents always accepted "I want to stay at my friends' place" as an okay reason for being out. But I was never out of my mind, and I always thought that God had his hand upon me.'

Tarsh's experience of God remained close throughout that year. She had a period of illness for some months and she suffered emotionally from worries about identity and image. 'God just spoke to me one day,' she remembers, 'with a quiet internal voice, and said, "Don't waste your life. Don't lose it. What are you doing to yourself? I want you to change." It was like I just woke up. I was doing little morning Bible studies for myself, and I'd say, "God, why am I doing this? Please help me." And he did.'

In her sixth year of high school, Tarsh made a new start. Her mother was living in Wellington and Tarsh went to live with her. But before long her mother headed further south, to Christchurch, in the South Island. Suddenly, the country girl from Tolaga Bay was a very long way from home, as she began her seventh year at Linwood High School. She did well enough there. An average student at the very least, she did well at sports and was always popular.

'But you couldn't help noticing how there were hardly any Maori in the general population. I was the only person doing Maori language as a subject and I had to do it by correspondence. For a girl from the East Coast, it was real culture shock. There were proportionately a lot more Maori in my church, a lot of them my own whanau and I helped run the youth group there. I was 17 by then and one of the oldest, but things weren't ideal there either, and it turned out that one of the married leaders was having an affair with one of the young girls. But God still had his hand on me-the first girl I met at Linwood High was another Christian and I remember consciously giving him thanks.'

At the end of the year, Tarsh went on to Canterbury University. This was a step she had never thought of taking and nor had any of her family-it represented new ground for all of them. She was excited about it all. One day, she was talking to the pastor at her church. His two sons had been at Canterbury and both had lost their Christian faith there. He said to her, 'The University will either strengthen your faith, or you'll lose it altogether.'

'I was determined,' Tarsh recalls. 'I couldn't see why an education and a faith couldn't live alongside each other. I joined the Christian Union and they were all pakeha-non-Maori New Zealanders-and middle class, but I could handle that better by then. They all thought intellectually about their faith and they applied it to different issues. That was just what I needed and I was into it.

'I have always had to be thoroughly involved in the things I do. So, for the time I was at University, I was in the Christian Union, on the Mission Committee, at Tertiary Students' Christian Fellowship conferences, leading cell groups and doing the Signpost Communications' Discovering Jesus course with inquirers. For three years, it was great. I learned so much about the faith, who Jesus is, how he relates to people and all kinds of pastoral issues. It was a real growing time of learning to love people.'

But the pace of it all was tiring for Tarsh and other big questions began to emerge. There was a split in her church the same year when one of the pastors tried to make it less Maori and into a more traditional Assemblies of God church. 'A lot of the Maori were offended,' Tarsh remembers, 'and the question really became, "What does it mean to be Christian? Do you have to do it in white style?" Because for me, I can't. I am a Christian; I'm also a Maori. How can I not be? It's out of the question for me to remove the Maori culture out of who I am—I couldn't, even if I wanted to. So how can I be truly Maori and truly Christian?'

At the end of that year, Tarsh went to a conference where she was the only Maori among 40 people who were discussing the question, 'How can we reach out to Maori?' They went on for a while before someone asked her what she thought. 'I said, "If you're going to reach out to Maori, you have to hang out with them, understand their culture and see how they move in their whanau. Relate to them and be among them. Do the structural stuff, but in the end, it comes down to relationships." '

But the group was not interested in what Tarsh had to say. 'I got burned,' she recalls. 'One guy said, "We don't want to hear about all that. We need to know what the steps are to take them the gospel-the one, two, three or whatever. We need to know how to do it." But I can tell you it doesn't happen that way, or not with Maori people. I doubt if it happens like that with anyone.'

Tarsh left the conference disillusioned, but the question remained with her of how to be authentically Maori and authentically Christian. She did Maori Honours in fourth year at university, and she was encouraged in the university Christian Fellowship group to take her faith to the same level as her studies.

'I became active in the Maori culture group, the University Kapa Haka Group and also in Te Akatoki, the Maori Students' Association. We wanted to establish the right for two Maori student representatives to sit on the University Students' Association and we had to fight for six hours to get a motion passed, in the face of constitutional legalists who looked suspiciously like racists. But what really challenged me was to wonder, "Where are the Christians to support my cause?" They weren't there. So what about Jesus' agenda, caring about the whole person and social justice and the kingdom on earth? How can evangelical Christians be separate from the political and the social? Some of our more liberal acquaintances have us beaten outright here.

'I'm not a radical. I'm just a young Maori person growing up in this Western, postmodern world and wanting to be real for Jesus in it. I want to see God's kingdom here on earth, not just a 'live-through-it-and-go-to-heaven' approach. I want to see God's justice done.'

Tarsh reflects on a Maori friend with a pakeha mother, who was brought up according to the standards of a middle-class white. 'Her parents are Christians and have been for years. She has become a lawyer, specialising on the Treaty of Waitangi-New Zealand's founding document-and she has thrown away her faith. She has done this because she cannot see Christianity fitting her life, because it is so mono-cultural and dominant. That hurts me. She's given up my God. If the church were, at heart, with Maori people for justice and human rights, more people would be interested in Jesus. It's not only Maori-indigenous people everywhere see the church as synonymous with colonisation-become Christian, become white. The connotations are negative, and the church has to get beyond them.

'So that's me. I've been working recently with a girls' home, with young High School girls at risk from tricky family situations. Most of them are abused in various ways. I believe Jesus wants us to show love to the homeless, the marginalised, the casualties of the successful society, those from other than good homes. It's not their fault. God has protected me and given me different opportunities. Many with similar backgrounds to mine have gone in very different ways.'

One of the first Maori Members of Parliament in New Zealand was Sir Apirana Ngata, who held a seat in the house for Eastern Maori from 1905 to 1935 and had a great effect on land reform. He was a lawyer with a concern for land reforms and a particular interest in preserving traditional Maori literature. He came from the area between Ruatoria and Tikitiki, the area of Tarsh Koia's whanau. His name is revered there still, and Ruatoria's high school is called Ngata Memorial College. He encouraged communal sheep farming among East Coast Maori, his wish being to ensure Maori adaptation to progressive ways. Tarsh quotes him as she reflects on her life:

'E tipu e rea mo nga ra o tou ao,
To ringa ki nga rakau a te Pakeha,
hei ara mo to tinana.

To ngakau ki nga taonga a o
tipuna Maori hei tikitiki mo tau mahuna.
To wairua ki te Atua nana nei nga mea katoa

Grow up and thrive for the days destined to you,
Your hand to the tools of the pakeha,
    to provide physical sustenance,
Your heart to the treasures of your Maori ancestors
    as a crown for your brow,
and your soul to God to whom
    all things belong.'

'This sums up my life. The university represents the good things of the pakeha. I am to live in this world and never forget I am Maori, remembering what my grandparents taught me, and theirs taught them, and my soul is God's. Pakeha tools for Maori people, and all under God. I have to work out what it means to be Maori and Christian in this day and age.'

Well, what made the difference?

Tarsh Koia has many reasons not to be a Christian. What factors helped her respond positively to God?

1. Tarsh got a distinctly uneasy feeling at the Jehovah's Witnesses Bible Study. Why do some people sense a dark, controlling spirituality where others, clearly, do not? In what way might God already be revealing himself to the young people we know?

2. School RE classes were important in teaching Tarsh truth. Are we using such channels to best effect? How could they be better supported and improved?

3. The concept of whanau is particularly significant for Tarsh and conveys an interconnectedness of family values and

beliefs more strongly than in most Western cultures. When ministering with adolescents, to what extent do we need to consider and involve their families?

4. Tarsh found much of church life to be patronising to Maori people. Yet she chose to stay. How can we better discover when the gospel turns from good news into a message of conformity? How can we identify the essence of the gospel and distinguish it from our social habits:

(a) for our own living

(b) for sensitive relations with other cultural groups?

almost without noticing

Gina Wong

'Where are you from?' people ask when they first meet. The question means different things to different people. Some tell you where they live, others where they grew up. Members of a different race or a person with an exotic accent may name their country of origin. The novelist Sylvia Ashton-Warner says, 'Accident of dwelling place does not necessarily mean parochialism of the soul.' Ask someone where 'home' is, and you are likely to be told where their dearest relatives live or where their most significant formative influences occurred.

So where is home for Gina Wong, an ethnic Malaysian Chinese? Although resident in New Zealand for over ten years, her earlier life was spent in Malaysia. Since arriving in New Zealand, she has lived in both Palmerston North and Wellington, and also in Dunedin.

Gina Wong is in her twenties. She found Christian faith in Kuala Lumpur when she was 14 years old. Her father retired as head of security for Shell Malaysia in 1995 but prior to this he was a ranking police officer. The family moved because of his work postings, shifting every three years. First located at Kuantan on the east coast, the family moved to Pahang, then to Raub in the central highlands during the communist insurgency in the early 1970s, to Ipoh some 150 kilometres north of Kuala Lumpur before a final posting to KL itself during the years between Gina's tenth and 15th birthdays.

Mr Wong had little faith in God. He was abandoned by his parents when he was a child, and ill-treated by his guardians.

On reaching adulthood, he became a police officer. While living in Raub on the edge of the jungle, he spent much of his time with the communists. As part of his job he found it necessary to befriend them to gain their cooperation. In the process, he was influenced by their disbelief in God. Gina's mother lived there in constant fear for her children's safety. Nowadays when Gina recalls Malaysia, she identifies it with Kuala Lumpur. She was 15 when she left for New Zealand.

Gina's mother was a member of a large family, living with her grandmother during her childhood. Next door lived a woman missionary who worked for the Baptist church in Kedah. She took the little girl under her wing and taught her to play the piano. Gina's mother loved music, going to church with the missionary and playing the piano there as well. She did this each week until she went away to nursing school. Then she lost contact with the church. Soon after this she married and had no real interest in belonging to a church until after their two children, Ron and Gina, were born.

When they were old enough for Sunday school, Gina's mother sent them along, as she wanted them to have Christian teaching. She believed Christianity had good moral values and social advantages, though she did not re-activate her own church links. The children went to Sunday school until Gina was seven or eight. When the family was moving around they gave it up as the children seemed too old for Sunday school and it became an effort to keep them there. Also, the Baptist church they attended became charismatic and Gina's mother was uneasy with this and thought it might be dangerous. Because her children had already received an early Christian education as she had done, it seemed all right for them to drift off.

Gina recalls the family's interests in the next few years as mostly focusing around material things. It remained this way until she was 13 or 14, when her brother Ron became a

Christian. His behaviour changed, and being close to him, she couldn't fail to notice.

Two factors influenced Ron's change of direction. Foremost was his friend Ivan, a young man with a strong Christian faith. Ivan's family also moved around in his early years, in similar places to the Wongs. As a consequence, the two boys grew up together, becoming good friends. Although they did not attend the same school, they travelled on the same school bus where their friendship developed. From time to time their conversations touched on areas of Ivan's faith and beliefs.

Sometimes, Ivan invited Ron to attend gospel crusades that were held once or twice a year at the local Catholic boys' school. The Christians there mounted a special evangelistic program of drama, singing and talks on the Christian message. The program was arranged and carried out by the senior students. They publicised their various acts and for an afternoon session were usually able to fill the hall. Because it was a close-knit school, they drew an audience of 500 or so, mostly made up of friends and friends of friends. The whole spectrum of religious backgrounds was represented-Catholics, Protestants, Eastern religions and materialists. Starting after the school's morning session the crusade finished during the afternoon shift. Younger students who attended school in the afternoon had their chance to attend the crusade in later years.

This local Christian event was socially acceptable among their peers, so it was easy for Ivan to ask Ron to attend. Among the bus gang they had many mutual friends and a high proportion of the 2,400 students from Ivan's school were in the audience. Through these gospel crusades and Ivan's friendship, Ron became a Christian at around the age of 15.

'He had been a black sheep,' Gina recalls. 'Although his best friend was a Christian, some of his other friends were quite roguish. Some of them had been caught shoplifting. He's a natural leader, but with that group at that time, he wasn't leading so much and he was starting to be led into things that weren't going to work out well for him. They were just into hedonism, really–anything for a good time.'

But suddenly things changed. Ron even changed his taste in music and started listening to Christian music. He kept the same friends, but he just stopped automatically doing everything they did.

Ivan belonged to the Assemblies of God church, which had an active youth group. When Ron also joined, a number of the young people began to spend time at the Wongs'. Sometimes Gina would go with Ron to the youth group's activities and she enjoyed their company. She could see where Ron's change of behaviour and outlook came from.

'His friends were always my friends and I wanted to know his new friends. We had a lot of good social times. I don't recall anyone talking about Christianity in any way that was significant to me then, but I definitely caught their friendly spirit and was really attracted to that. Ron often used to talk to me about Christianity. He used to come in and tell me my music was evil. I mean, it was standard 1980s pop music–there wasn't anything special about it–but Ron said it was evil. He said that I should be listening to Christian music and introduced me to some of his. I didn't like it much.'

Gina didn't want to listen to Ron's music, especially after he was so pushy about it. But she would get curious over what was so special about it and would sometimes listen to it after he went out. One night, Ron came home and talked for hours about the people at the youth group and the Christian faith. Then he asked her if she had considered becoming a Christian. 'If it came down to it,' Gina says, 'I couldn't tell a Christian from a non-Christian. But I liked the people I knew were his good friends and it seemed all right. So when he asked me if I wanted to become a Christian I said, "I don't see why not." He prayed a prayer with me and I went off to bed. It was quite late-say, 3.00 am.

'I didn't realise this was such a significant thing until the next day. I accepted it in blind faith, not from any great convincing thing. But the next day one of our friends said to me, "Terrific news about last night. You're a Christian now," and I thought, "Wow, I didn't realise it was such a big deal. This must be significant." He was quite excited, much more than I was, and I thought it must be quite important. When I look back, I see that his excitement was quite important to my understanding.'

Gina began attending Ron's youth group along with their friends. It met on a Friday night. As neither of their parents attended church, it took a while for Gina's parents to realise it also had a Sunday component. The Kuala Lumpur Assemblies of God church is a large group, with over 1500 people. When Ron and Gina wanted to extend their allegiance into Sunday services, their mother went along a few times to check it out. Discovering its charismatic ways brought back ten-year-old memories of the Baptist church that had alarmed her earlier, and she said she didn't want them to go to 'that sort of church'. Her husband supported this stance, and for quite a while they were limited to Friday and the youth group.

'But Mum noticed a change in us,' Gina says. 'We became closer than we had been and we spent less time fighting. Ron has always been protective of me, but we used to have our moments. But here we had this common problem, of no church, only youth group, and we were wondering, "How can we convince our parents?" The answer we thought of was to obey them. So we set about doing this and it drew us closer together. They weren't used to us being so obedient, so they were impressed. Then, they relented about church. It was gradual at first-once a month, no more. But it became okay and we were finally allowed to go whenever.

'Eventually Mum came along, too. She was impressed by the acceptance we found in the church, and not just among our age group. She knew all our friends, who used to come around our house a lot, and she liked them. She came more and more frequently, and gradually grew into a faith of her own. My dad has never been fully convinced-he's come to the odd special event, but he's never become a regular church attender.'

Circumstances may have played a part in all this. Ron went with Ivan, Gina went with Ron, Mrs Wong went with the children. But not too long after, all the family moved to New Zealand for the sake of the children's education and future, except for Mr Wong. Moving to Wellington in 1989, they were joined by their father only after he retired in 1995.

At present, the family live in a Wellington suburb. Following completion of her high schooling at Wellington's Newlands College, Gina spent four years in Palmerston North, studying at Massey University. She began studying veterinary science because she liked animals and carried on for three years because she kept passing the course requirements. However, increasingly she did not feel cut out for this course and switched to psychology in 1995. The change gave her access to Wellington's Victoria University, and later to Otago University, Dunedin.

But the time at Massey made sense out of a previous experience that had occurred to her in Kuala Lumpur. Massey University is situated on the outskirts of Palmerston North, a provincial centre set among fertile grasslands in rich dairy and mixed farming country, the antithesis of the large, bustling, cosmopolitan, high-rise city of Kuala Lumpur. The centre of the town is dominated by a garden square and the whole place is flat. Established first as a farming research centre, it later grew to full university status. Keen westerly winds move through Palmerston North, contrasting with the tropical 'closeness' of Kuala Lumpur's climate.

One day, Gina recalled a frighteningly vivid dream, occurring a fortnight after she became a Christian. She had been certain it was significant, but didn't understand what it was about. Her brother was unable to help her, seeing no meaning in something that was extremely significant to her.

In the dream, she found herself leading a group of frightened people through tall buildings. Then she came out into green hills, brilliant, grassy and clear. It did not add up to anything she recognised or could make sense of. Five years later, she was struck by a comment by her flat mate, that dreams are often significant and may involve the future. Now within the green landscape of New Zealand, her dream hit home.

Gina completed her degree at the end of 1997 and went on to Dunedin to do a post-graduate Diploma in Clinical Psychology. Ron has also completed an Information Systems degree. Her father has retired, while her mother is a principal nurse at a Wellington hospital. Gina has been associated with Wellington's Lifepoint Assemblies of God church and with the University's Overseas Christian Fellowship, a group of 25-30 students. She first heard of this fellowship from friends on holiday while she was living in Kuala Lumpur and decided then to join them if she ever had the chance. She finds it hard to accept the looser Christian commitment of the Western church, which is too swayed by social trends around it. When Gina came to faith she did not realise the extent of what she had taken on. She is increasingly determined to make available the depths of what she has learned about faith to others. The OCF has given her an avenue to help strengthen the commitment of those close to her.

well, what made the difference?

The details of Gina Wong's life suggest these key events to her finding faith:

1. She was favourably impressed by her impressions of Christianity as given by her brother and his friends. How can we encourage our young people to be consistent in their conduct and favourable in their impressions? Is the challenge greater at home?

2. There came a day when Gina's brother, Ron, put a specific challenge to commitment in front of her. It does not seem to have been ideally timed, but it played a role. Are we too often cautious about being deliberate in our calls for response? What are the right times?

3. Her brother's friend's excited response to her new faith, brittle though that faith was, was also significant to her. How can we better allow an appropriate enthusiasm for Christian development to become part of our daily approach?

4. The teaching Gina received at youth group and church reinforced the early steps. How can we contribute to good teaching on an on-going basis?

singing and dancing
Ron Tevita

The name of Ron Tevita still sticks in the mind of his deputy principal at Porirua College, a school on the outskirts of Wellington, New Zealand. He also remembers a particular end of year junior school prize-giving for the same reason, as he was the master of ceremonies.

The principal had asked the music department to perform some musical items as part of the program. 'We had the opening ceremonials,' the deputy principal recalls, as if it were yesterday. 'The teaching staff were all dressed up in their finery and we'd awarded some of the prizes. We were up to what was listed as a musical item: "Ron Tevita, solo, All Over Me." I didn't know any song by that name-I didn't know Ron Tevita either, although I'd heard he could sing a bit.'

But when he looked at this song title he wondered, 'Whatever are we in for here?' End of year school programs can end up with all sorts of material and he thought this might be some sort of seedy love song. 'I nearly made a smart remark before he started singing to show that we weren't going to be taken too much by surprise if it turned out to be risqué or anything. I didn't make any actual comment. I read his name and paused a bit and gave a silly sort of emphasis to the song title just to imply that anything might happen.

'Then I got out of his way and he picked up the microphone. Well, it wasn't a seedy love song. It turned out to be a Christian song about the blood of Jesus. The theme was that the singer was covered by the sacrifice, by the blood-that it was "all over me", and that there was nothing else to offer God. He sang it so simply and so profoundly that the whole assembly hall was absolutely still when he finished. They were slow to applaud-it was like church. And when it was over, I remember thinking, "So what do I say now? Junior long jump awards?" I actually paused for a few seconds, to let the silence speak for itself and said, "Thank you Ron". Whatever the next comment was, it was going to seem out of place, like interrupting a prayer to ask about the cleaning roster. Ron nearly ruined the prize-giving.'

It was not that the school was unused to Christian songs on its public programs. The area has a high percentage of Pacific Island families, many with church backgrounds. It was not his choice of song that was so remarkable but the vulnerability of his performance that, for a moment, lifted the award ceremony into a much higher realm.

Ron's parents, David and Sera Tevita, were one among many families who journeyed from Western Samoa to Wellington in 1970. If you look back over New Zealand's immigration history, what marks the late 1960s is the large influx of permanent residents from the Pacific Islands. Today, when looking at the country's social groupings, the Polynesian community is a visible component. No one watching an All Black rugby team can fail to notice the number of Islanders playing at the country's highest level.

David and Sera Tevita had four sons when they arrived in Wellington. Two more sons were born over the next two or three years. By then the family had moved to Porirua, a satellite suburb 15 to 20 kilometres north of Wellington. The suburb was barely established in 1960, but as a number of immigrant families took advantage of the extensive government housing provided there, it grew rapidly over the next decade.

The Tevita family started attending the Porirua East Baptist Church about two years after their move to Wellington, soon after their arrival in Porirua. Like many Pacific Islanders, they had a long tradition of church attendance. They respected greatly their clergy, viewing them as authority figures. An early priority after their arrival in New Zealand was to locate an appropriate church. A number of large Pacific Island churches of various denominations have formed through the Islanders' desire to establish familiar patterns of church structure and practices in the new country, and the Tevitas joined one of these.

But a curious incident paved the way to their move to the Baptist church. Since arriving in New Zealand, David Tevita had worked in various jobs at places like Ford Motors and Ashley Wallpapers. On this particular day he had gone to bed to catch up on some sleep before the night shift. He asked the boys to tell any visitors he was unavailable because he needed the sleep.

As it happened, the minister of their Pacific Island church chose to make a pastoral call that day. When the children told him their father's message, the pastor responded, 'Say it's the minister.' Rightly or wrongly, David Tevita took this to be an insensitive appeal to traditional authority. Now experiencing the relative freedom of New Zealand society, and with less than a total commitment to the church and what it stood for, he decided to leave the church in question. At the time he was playing in a band and another band member took him along to the Baptist church. This association continued for many years.

Ron, born in 1973, was the youngest by two years of the six Tevita boys and eight years younger than his oldest brother, Manu. As he grew up, he attended Cannons Creek Primary School, then Brandon Intermediate and Porirua College. His links with the church, now known as the Hosanna Fellowship, continued. He is now in his twenties, still part of the church, acknowledging the central role it has played in his journey into Christian faith.

The church has a performing arts group called JAM, which stands for Jesus and Me. Their speciality is music and dance, and they first got together in the mid-1980s to do items at events such as Youth for Christ rallies. JAM started to build up a bit of a name and the items they performed began to be the main reason for them coming together, and they reached a point where many of the group had either stopped attending Hosanna Fellowship or had never done so.

Gary Colville joined the church as a pastor around this time. The group had become pretty independent but Gary was very supportive of them. He approached them one day to see if they could be a part of the church, and he asked them why they weren't Christians. They gave their various reasons, including saying that some church people looked pretty good on Sundays but didn't look so good on the other days. To them, these people weren't too different from the JAM team, except they were in the church and the JAM people weren't.

Gary Colville thought about this for a while then gave them another challenge. He told them to go away and consider whether this was a good enough reason to reject God. The group took up the challenge and, when they had considered the question, decided they could not think of any valid reasons for rejecting God. They told the pastor this and he decided to do them a deal.

The deal was simple enough. The group could stick around the church so long as, whenever they met for practice or performance, one of them prayed. In return for this concession to the parent body, the pastor contracted to mind their administrative affairs and be their manager. The group had had trouble filling this role and as the Christian expression required wasn't onerous, they agreed to the terms. One or two were doubtful, but they stayed on.

Ron was too young to be involved at this time, but he remembers it because three of his brothers were in the band. In due course, most of the members of the group became Christians, simply by being in, around and part of the church.

In 1987, just before Ron turned 14, he joined the group. This was his first year at Porirua College, and he became associated with the youth group through his oldest brother, Manu, who had been going to the church ever since the pastor put the challenge to JAM. But what Ron really remembers is the change in Manu over this time. 'Our family is a quiet family,' he explains, 'and Manu an especially quiet member of it. But there had always been an anger in him. In Samoan families, there is a strong authority thing-the father has great control over the family and young people are expected to respect older people. In our family of six boys, the oldest one had to help show authority for the younger ones. So Manu was linked in to all that because he was the oldest. Also, he was older than the rest of the brothers when the family came to New Zealand and he was the most affected by the language problems. It couldn't have been easy for him.'

But Ron remembers that one day the 'anger just melted away. There was a change inside him. He just looked like he had some kind of peace. The next thing was that he started to ask us if we wanted to go to the youth group with him. There were these study groups on Tuesday nights and after a while I felt sorry for him because none of us would go with him. So one day I said I would, and I went along.

'I felt comfortable enough about being there. I knew everybody from church because we always went on Sundays. I knew the songs, too, so it was easy enough for me to fit into it. The study was led by the pastor for perhaps six months or so. Then he divided the group into smaller groups and got the youth group members to lead these. The larger group was growing because others brought along their family or friends. There was a good, group feeling that made people want to stay and bring others along. JAM was part of it and that was another attraction.'

Ron went along to their performances, hesitantly at first but increasingly fascinated. He could see that what the group was doing was powerful. The group performed at a number of youth rallies and at a couple of Christian music festivals. Opportunities to perform grew, coming from a variety of sources. In fact, there were so many that the pastor had to vet their invitations. He ensured, before agreeing to perform at a specific Christian function, that certain criteria were in place. He did not want them to burn out for causes they could no longer identify with.

Ron joined JAM soon after Manu took him along to the Tuesday night group. At the time he wasn't a Christian, although he was 'learning to be one. When I joined JAM, God was already part of my background and the Tuesday night teaching at the youth group was helpful, as well as my brother's example. I guess I was starting to feel that if there could be changes in my brother, maybe there could also be changes in me. I'm not sure exactly when I consciously knew I believed in Jesus. It kind of grew in me as an understanding. But I do remember a day when I decided to state that I was a believer.

'It was a Sunday, at church. I couldn't tell you what the sermon was about. But at the end, there was an invitation from our pastor to come forward for prayer. He often did that but I remember that day deciding, deliberately, that I was going to go forward and receive prayer. I believed, but I'd never actually said so, and I knew I was going up that day. My thoughts were along the lines of, "Today is the day I state it." There was nothing spectacular in what happened, just me finding a way to say, "Yes, now I know I'm a Christian."

'My father is also a Christian now. He wasn't when he first went to the Baptist church, all those years ago. But neither of my parents ever had any question about the reality of God. God was always there in their minds. It was more a matter of how they related to him. There are strong church ties in Samoan culture and people expect to go to church on Sunday. As well, my parents always wanted to keep up our religious activities. So we used to have the Samoan Bible readings and hymns. Everyone had a turn at the readings, then we'd sing some praise songs and have a prayer time. We always tried to keep to this pattern, even before the family became Christians.'

As Ron's commitment to the church and JAM increased, so did his performing abilities. A year or two after he produced his knock-out school assembly performance, he sang in a duet on a commercial recording produced jointly by his school and a neighbouring one. The tape included a variety of songs such as 'Tuxedo Junction' and 'Wind Beneath My Wings', and Ron and his partner provided 'Cool Rain', a song about the Holy Spirit.

When Ron left school in 1991, he achieved his desire to work full-time with the church. His two main roles were as a leader of worship and as part of the creative arts ministry. Since then, he has finished a computing course at Whitireia Polytech in Porirua and he is now engaged in computer work in Wellington.

It might seem a bit strange that all these changes in Ron and his family came about partly because a pastor insisted on waking a man sleeping before the night shift. But through the hand of God, small events can echo for generations. And like the performance of Ron Tevita at that school presentation, the sounds of these echoes can leave equally lasting impressions.

well, what made the difference?

1. Two factors gave Ron Tevita an advantage. One was his family's long-term association with a local church; the other, the traditional family acceptance of theological principles. But then he had to make them personal. How did this come about?

2. The change he observed in his brother Manu was clearly influential. In fact, many of the stories within this book examine the power of transformed lives. But are they powerful only when someone recognises that they need to be transformed, also?

3. The powerful influence of JAM gave Ron an outlet for his artistic abilities, linked to deliberate Christian living. How important is it to the wholeness that the gospel brings that people's gifts, skills and abilities find a place for their expression?

4. The Tevita family's Samoan culture had a very strong tradition of church attendance. Yet the family all came to recognise that this wasn't enough. Such traditions can provide a form for spirituality. Can they ever pass on the need for a more personal encounter with God?

honouring your father
Iris Lee

Casey and Carmen Lee of Kuala Lumpur discovered soon after their conversion that they couldn't have both their faith and the respect of their parents. This Malaysian couple of Chinese origin comes from a Taoist-Confucianist tradition that emphasises ancestor worship. And for Casey's parents, the couple's Christianity didn't just threaten the family's culture, history and tradition-it threatened their place in the after-life, along with that of all their ancestors.

To the Christian with little knowledge of this tradition, ancestor-worship is viewed as putting the ancestor in the place of Jesus. To people following the tradition, the belief is that the ancestors pass into an after-life with a status which is affected by how much reverence is shown by their descendants. These descendants often choose to worship a variety of deities to cover their options for eternity, but they will ensure that their ancestors are among them, in order to cover theirs.

Depending on the emphasis of the chosen beliefs, the after-life may have components of both reincarnation and heaven. At a funeral, descendants of the deceased may make a variety of ritual sacrifices. They believe the spirits will change these sacrifices into benefits for the deceased in the after-life. So when offering a sacrifice, it is an advantage to have a variety of objects of worship. If you do not include your parents, they are disadvantaged.

Those who are part of the Taoist-Confucian tradition understand these nuances. If a person becomes more reverent in their worship, no one over-reacts, even if the person pulls back from some aspect of belief or takes on a previously unnoticed deity. The strength or poverty of a person's devotion is not a subject of comment. Yet when Iris Lee's parents became Christians when she was ten, the harmony of the family's life was seriously shaken.

On the surface, this change should have made little difference to the family. Taoism-Confucianism is sufficiently fluid to allow the addition of gods from various sources. But Lee's relatives lost tolerance for the family members when their own place in the after-life was threatened.

It was harder for Iris's father's family to accept than for her mother's. Casey Lee's family devoutly followed the ancestral belief system and expected his allegiance. But they also expected his wife's allegiance. A daughter marries into her husband's family and is expected to be a filial daughter, following their practices. She must worship the ancestors of her husband, not those of her original family. It was a bitter thing to be told by their son that he and his wife had renounced what they had been brought up to respect. After raising him to respect his elders, as they had learned to respect theirs, this was their reward. Even if Casey had become a more loving member of the family since professing his faith in Jesus Christ, this belief deprived them of their salvation. There was now no one to care for their interests in the future life.

Iris's parents found Christianity in their mid-30s. When Iris was five years old, the family moved from Kuala Lumpur to a place in the country, about 40 kilometres south. Casey believed that there they could more easily find the peace and security he was seeking to unite the family.

This was not a silly idea, for whatever Kuala Lumpur's other attractions, its admirers would be unlikely to describe it as a city of peace. It has a population of over 1.3 million and government policy makes it possible for everyone to own a car. It has become a city of motorways, traffic and high rise buildings. Malaysia produces a 'people's car' and tollgates fund the operations of its various motorways. If you leave before six in the morning, it takes 20 minutes to travel from Kajang, the suburban area where Iris's family lived, to downtown Kuala Lumpur. Any later and the 35 kilometre journey takes over an hour. Temperatures are usually 30° Celsius and the climate is humid. Flooded roads can delay traffic for hours. The city is busy, exciting and prosperous . . . but not synonymous with peace

Iris's parents did not find peace and serenity in this more rural atmosphere. Nagging fears began to permeate their busy working lives and they started to question their family religious traditions. Casey wondered: 'So someone dies-you pray for them to reach heaven safely and that the spirits will sort out their possessions. But what if people don't pray enough or they make the wrong sacrifices? Will the spirits sort out the possessions? Can you trust them? How can you tell?' Even the most devout people, he wondered, did not have an antidote for this fear. There had to be a better way.

The Lees made friends in Kajang with a couple who happened to pastor a church there. So they started to visit the church on a Sunday-partly out of politeness, partly out of curiosity. From the outset, they discovered real warmth, even though they were only visitors. They gained the impression that they were not being assessed for what they could do and the Christian friends they made there became very important to them.

Soon after, Casey gradually began accepting the claims of Jesus, and made a decision to follow him. However, he still had trouble believing that God could really love him, though this was to change quite miraculously. Casey had a compressed disc between his lower vertebrae which touched the nerves and began to interfere with his muscular control. Sometimes, he lost control of his left leg altogether when it would suddenly give way. He was advised to undergo corrective surgery. Putting off this decision, his condition deteriorated.

During this period he was invited to attend a Miracle Rally in Petaling Jaya. On the second day he hobbled along there, as much to please the pastor as anything else, and because transport there was free. The preacher from Singapore was completely unknown to Casey, yet he amazed him by giving an exact description of his medical condition and inviting the man fitting this description to come forward for God to heal him. Casey went forward and was healed. His doubts about God's love and care dissolved immediately.

Iris's mother, Carmen, witnessed a similar miraculous event. Just two months after she decided to follow Jesus, her car was stolen. A few days later, after the police had given up hope of finding it, she experienced a vision of a row of trees and a roadside food stall. As she prayed, she felt an urge to leave the house immediately. Carmen borrowed a car-not knowing where she was going-and headed off, guided by the prompting of the Spirit. She soon found herself in an unfamiliar part of town that she recognised as the scene of her vision. And there also, she recognised her lost car, abandoned but undamaged.

The family experienced a variety of these kinds of incidents-and also some very creepy occurrences. On one occasion, all the fish in the pond disappeared unaccountably and a number of their dogs suddenly died. Then ticks appeared all over the walls of their home, which could not be made to leave until Carmen and Casey prayed for them to go.

Iris was ten in this first year of the family's Christian involvement. All the family was drawn into the life of the church. 'We didn't all understand Christianity the same way,' Iris remembers, 'but we were all involved. The church fellowship didn't have its own building, so we had to set it up each week-putting out the chairs, the overhead projector, tidying up and other jobs. My sister, Doris, is 22 months older than me. She got busy and so did I. And all the time the teaching was happening, and I began to understand about Christianity quite a lot.

'You'd have called us a Christian family then. And my grandparents certainly called us that. They didn't approve at all. They were very upset with their children. To leave your ancestor worship was very disrespectful to your parents.'

The Kajang church comprised perhaps 40 or 50 people. Some university students attended whom the children affectionately called 'uncle' and 'aunt'. The small congregation produced a real family atmosphere, Iris recalls. 'We knew the pastor well-you knew everybody.'

The church focused very strongly on teaching. 'But, for a long time, while I understood about Christianity, I didn't understand you had to respond yourself. One day, when I was about 12, the pastor came to talk to me. I wasn't surprised. She would often talk to people she thought needed special help, even if they hadn't looked for it. She had asked my parents first and it was all very appropriate. She came to me and we talked for a while. Then she asked me if I wanted to respond to Jesus myself. We were just on our own, but it wasn't threatening. She was close to us all and I knew her well. She explained how we needed to approach Jesus ourselves and she led me in a confession prayer.'

Iris describes that day as her conversion, when her understanding transformed into commitment. At 13, she was in high school. Her school had originally been established by nuns from the Catholic Church and was still called Kajang Convent Secondary School. But since Malaysia's independence from the

British, the language of instruction had changed from English to Malay. The government had taken over the funding and operation of the school and it became a government school on private land.

There was a small Christian Fellowship at the school. Iris describes it as 'underground', not recognised as an official school activity. Extra-curricular and voluntary activities existed, with a variety of sporting and other clubs. But the Christian Fellowship was secretive, with no posters or announcements of activities.

In Muslim Malaysia, the government is anything but enthusiastic about such groups, especially in a Malay school. Malays are not allowed to convert to Christianity and a Malay Christian is officially a contradiction in terms. However, there are Malaysian Christians. The ethnic blend of the population is roughly 60 per cent Malay, 30 per cent Chinese and 10 per cent Indian. These groupings reflect the country's chequered history; various workers from different nationalities have been brought in at different times. The Malays, who are Muslims, are vigorously unsympathetic to Christians. Only one school in the district of Hulu Langat is thought to have an officially recognised Christian organisation, although the universities have such groups, and private institutions do not need government approval.

Over the next couple of years, Iris's Christian growth continued. At the age of 18 she was awarded a scholarship from the Singaporean government to study in Singapore. She spent the next 18 months there, finishing off her schooling prior to university. It was a bigger school than she was used to, with over a thousand students. Many were on scholarships or pursuing the school's streamed education. Iris did well, thriving on the enhanced educational opportunities and living in a student hostel.

She moved to New Zealand in 1996 at the age of 19, when awarded a scholarship to study commerce at Wellington's Victoria University. Her sister Doris was also in New Zealand, studying accountancy at Waikato University, six hours by car from Wellington. The Overseas Christian Fellowship (OCF) nurtured the two sisters in their student days and they were able to meet up at its national conferences. Iris lived close to the University in a Christian hostel for overseas students in her first year at University, before moving out into a flat.

Having completed a BCA degree, Iris now works in Enterprise Risk Services for the accountancy and management consultancy firm, Deloitte Touche Tohmatsu. Her flatmates, a group called Oasis, are involved in urban mission, working with new immigrants. Her church is Lifepoint, a Wellington charismatic fellowship. Iris retains close links with the OCF.

Iris's path to faith originated in her father Casey's determination to trust in Jesus' word that he was 'the way, the truth and the life' and that the only way to the God the Father was through him, without the need for the prayers of his ancestors or children. Even though Casey's parents were mortified that their son was not honouring his father, in a deeper sense he was doing exactly that-honouring his new Father in heaven and the message he sent through his son Jesus.

And this has become Iris's mission, also. From that heady first year at the Kajang church to her prayer of commitment with the pastor, Iris has been discovering more of 'the way, the truth and life' that Jesus brings, and how to share this with others.

well, what made the difference?

For Iris Lee, the pathway to Christian faith was closely linked to her family. What can we learn from Iris's story?

1. Her family was greatly influenced by miraculous experiences of God. What are the tensions involved in seeing these events as either a regular part of Christianity, or rare, exceptional events?

2. Iris's involvement in church life gave her ways of serving through a variety of tasks such as setting up the church every week in its borrowed premises. How can people be given avenues of service within the church while not letting them simply feel used in the process?

3. The direct challenge by the Kajang church pastor who knew and understood Iris's situation brought about her Christian commitment. Because of the close, family nature of the church this was not threatening to Iris. How can these situations remain unthreatening within larger churches, or where there is less familiarity?

4. Iris's family's Christian commitment was inevitably threatening to Casey's parents. Similar situations have happened since the time of Jesus. But would every effort to 'honour' Casey's parents compromise his Christianity?

belief, faith and modelling
Charlie Farmery

Charlie Farmery has never had trouble believing the teachings of Christianity. But that mystical journey of seeing belief grow into faith has for him been a long and almost imperceptible series of small but profound insights.

In his early teens Charlie attended a church camp. There was a boy called Terry who had come alone, without friends. It didn't look as if he would make any friends over the weekend either, because he was 'pretty clumsy and not very socially skilled'.

On Saturday afternoon, everyone was trying to get Terry to have a ride on an aerial trapeze. But he didn't want to and began to get upset. 'I didn't blame him,' says Charlie. 'It was pretty frightening and he wasn't very good at that sort of thing. But Peter Hyatt, the group leader, really wanted to make it easier for this boy, and got us all to encourage him and applaud him-even prayed with us that he'd have the courage to launch out.'

Well, Terry made it on the aerial trapeze that day and the experience transformed both him and the attitude to him of the other boys at the camp. For Charlie it was an example of faith in action that has stayed with him ever since.

But Charlie's story starts in the village of Potten End. This village is located just out of Berkhamsted between Hemel Hamstead and Aylesbury in Hertfordshire, just half an hour's drive north west of London.

Charlie's parents, Keith and June Farmery, have lived in the area for years. Keith is a banker and June a homemaker. They have three children, Carolyn, Neil and Charlie, their youngest. The Farmerys were part of the Potten End Anglican church until Charlie and Neil were six and eight years old. Then they made a move to the more visibly evangelical Sunnyside Church in Berkhamsted, which had a Sunday school and youth group activities for the children.

'Not that it was high drama,' says Charlie. 'It had a Sunday school but it wasn't Star Trek or anything. I used to go along and sit down and mostly behave myself, but I thought it was pretty dull.'

Charlie believed what was taught there. He thought that everyone else believed the same as the teachers and found it boring going over things they already believed. Besides, being in middle school, the transition between primary and secondary school in the English education system at the time, he remembers that 'all I was really worried about was playing a lot of football'.

'For me, school went on at one level and church went on at another, with not a lot of places for the two to meet. School could be quite rough at times, with bullying here and there. It didn't leap out at a kid as an obvious climate where Sunday school teaching would flower.'

When he was ten Charlie began to attend Pathfinders, a church-based group for 10-14 year olds. It usually met on Sunday mornings while adult church programs were in progress. At Sunnyside, 20 or 25 young people met in the churchwarden's house. Jenny and Peter Hyatt, the program's leaders, intentionally designed the group to think about the Christian faith and created a place where friends who didn't come from a Christian background could feel comfortable.

Charlie reacted well to the Pathfinder model. 'You were treated as someone a bit more mature,' he said. 'Not quite as an adult.

But you were looked on as someone expected to think a bit, rather than just sitting and absorbing things. Seeing what Christianity meant to other people was very important, too. Jenny and Peter were right into it and you wanted to know what its meaning really was.'

Charlie could see that Christianity was much more than an idea to some of the people in the group, and he decided to pursue this difference further. 'Here were people my age, and others I respected, talking about how Christianity meant something to them. So I started to develop some questions of my own. In terms of faith, if we can use that word to describe the things we believe, I never found any of it very difficult to get a hold on. I believed that Jesus was who he said he was and I believed in God and heaven and hell-all the theology was sort of inbred and I never actually doubted it. If anyone questioned things at the level of fundamental doubt, I felt a strange feeling inside, wondering 'Why are you questioning that?' But for faith to mean, not just belief, but making a difference to living, well, I found that much more remote.'

It was about this time that Charlie attended the camp with Terry. This and many other events produced a deep wonder within him about how these ideas he had always believed had the power to transform lives.

Charlie continued to attend Pathfinders' camps. When he was 13 he attended a summer camp at Sidmouth called Venture Holidays, run by the Anglican Church Pastoral Aid Society (CPAS). Sidmouth is a sleepy town on England's south coast. CPAS took over a local school for ten days with access to all the school's grounds and leisure facilities as well as its dormitories. Between 70 and 80 young people attended, with 24 leaders.

Among the activities was a game called Hunt the Leader. The leaders disappeared into Sidmouth disguised as local citizens, waiting to be discovered by campers who then scored points for recognising them. For this activity, Jenny and Peter dressed up as punks with crazy make-up, spiked hair and studs. They then hid themselves in a bus shelter among a group of old ladies. None of the campers was game enough to get close.

Jenny and Peter's influence was refreshing and challenging for Charlie. Their attractive, extroverted personalities, integrated with a sincere faith, provided an attractive role model. And their ability to help people discover Christianity for themselves challenged Charlie's perceptions of his faith without patronising him. At Sidmouth, most of these leaders were students-close enough in age to relate to the campers but old enough to still appear sophisticated.

Near the end of the Sidmouth camp, the leaders provided a time for people to ask God to enter their lives. 'And I just did that,' says Charlie. 'It didn't seem to make an immediate difference. I felt peaceful and quite happy that I'd done it. There was nothing spectacular about it. I had gone to the camp with two friends and they responded in a similar way. We were all at the same stage, I suppose. It was the first time we'd ever consciously listened and considered how faith might be relevant to us. It was really good to have them there. A lot of times we'd all just be sitting around or lying on our beds just chatting through what we actually believed. It was really good.'

Charlie remembers that the leaders seemed to be able to relate to the 'remote faith that I had in my head' and encourage it to bloom. Jenny and Peter were also to have an important role as his faith developed after the camp. They had heard about Charlie's commitment through his dormitory leader, and later from him, but were not involved at the time. They would be able to help Charlie discover the meaning of this commitment and think through the teaching he heard at the camp.

Charlie was on a high for a couple of weeks following the camp, as many people find after friendships are made and relationships deepened while on holiday. But close friends probably did not notice any difference in him. He didn't make any announcements to his family. 'But then, I never really would have told them anything like that,' he says. 'I didn't really tell anybody much-I wasn't really close to anyone that I would have trusted things like that to. The school scene was rough and aggressive, and didn't lend itself to talking much about yourself, though I probably told the people I went on the camp with, and a fair number in the Pathfinder group.'

The next four or five years Charlie describes as 'a bit of a roller-coaster ride'. He didn't go back to Sidmouth, but for the next five summers he went to St Anne's, a camp just outside Blackpool. He would go there every year and be on a high, 'then I'd go home and basically crash or at least stagger a bit. But I'd always attend the Pathfinder group or the youth group and try to keep some semblance of something going. I was useless at Bible reading-and still am. I didn't do it very often unless someone led us in the youth group. I did pray a fair bit, although it seemed a bit impersonal at the time. Looking back, though, I'm glad I was praying, even if it did vary a lot. But the camp helped to keep me going.'

However, the camps did more than just keep Charlie going. As he returned regularly over the years to the camp at St Anne's with his two friends, he progressively took on more responsibility. They began as cleaners or kitchen assistants and gradually became more involved helping with group Bible studies and assisting the dormitory leaders.

During his final years at High School, at the ages of 16 and 17, Charlie's faith progressed as he helped lead his local Pathfinder group. 'Not spectacularly-even slowly-but it did progress. Taking a position of responsibility and actually doing something for

God was good. It was a very gradual process, but doing something constructive at St Anne's and with the Pathfinders group was helpful. My lower sixth form year was dominated by a girlfriend who ended up dumping me, but my faith helped me in that, too. I can see God really moved there. She and I had both been helping the youth leader with the Pathfinders, so it was all mixed up together.'

The other significant thing that year was Charlie's confirmation service, which came the week before his A-levels, the final series of high school examinations that determine which educational institutions will accept you.

His confirmation service came at a significant time in his life. 'It was the first time I'd ever felt any insecurity in my life. I was at the height of worrying about what I was going to do–the universities I wanted to go to hadn't replied to my application and I'd got offers from places I really didn't want to attend. It was all very confusing.'

But then, half way through his confirmation service, a woman started speaking out in the church saying that she felt God wanted Charlie to know something. She didn't know me well enough to know what was going on in my life so it was even more special to me when she said, 'I feel God really wants to say to you that he is leading you, he's got his hand on your life and he'll take you wherever he wants you to go.' This was very helpful for me to hear at the time. It made me cry. It really signalled to me that what she asked for me was going to happen.

'I'd been a bit doubtful about this confirmation service beforehand. Not about getting confirmed as such–I was clear about that–but about the actual service. I thought it might be a bit stuffy or even off-putting with the bishop there and all the church style. I was more used to something informal. So it was even more special to have this lady say her thing during the service. Then, when my A-level results came out, I missed out on a B grade by 0.14 percent. This actually gave me freedom to steer away from a couple of places I didn't want to attend. I ended up at Southampton and I believe God wanted me there. That has since motivated me to make Christianity a really big part of my life at university.'

At Southampton University, Charlie completed a degree in Modern History and Politics. There he always tried to make his faith central to his decision making. He led group Bible studies in his university hall and he and a friend shared leadership of a group of half a dozen students. In conversations with fellow students he often found himself quietly challenging them about their relationship with God.

After finishing university, Charlie started teacher training but dropped out. Now in his 20s, he works part-time for a removal company. There he is able to share his faith with the other men. While sorting out what he wants to do long term he is being greatly used in his church youth group. His fellow leaders admire his skills, seeing him as a towering role model to the young people coming through the church.

Whatever direction his life takes from here, there will always be opportunities for him to see his belief transform into faith, his faith produce love and that love transform others, because Charlie has already discovered it does this in his own life.

well, what made the difference?

1. Charlie describes the Pathfinders' leaders as being a very influential example of faith to him. Yet he describes himself as being very closed and hesitant to talk about spiritual matters with others during this period of his life. How might

Jenny and Peter have known what influence their teaching had on him? How much would have been done without knowing its effects?

2. Charlie always came back from the camps, on a spiritual high, yet he crashed soon after. Is there any significant relationship between the 'spiritual high' of camp and its lasting effects? Why do some spiritual highs produce lasting effects and others not?

3. The clear call at camp to make a decision to follow God was another turning point for Charlie. What difference did it make in his life? And did he understand its significance?

4. Taking up opportunities for Christian ministry can be formative in the faith journey of young people. Charlie was motivated to take God more seriously after beginning to lead groups. What factors enable a person to 'live up to' the responsibility they have been given?

5. Charlie's journey to faith came through a series of small revelations, yet many of us become frustrated when we do not see these small revelations lead to a major conversion. If faith can be both an event and a process, how can we respect the work of God and not force part of a process into being 'the event'?

one hour Christians
Adele Ross

It would not be surprising if Adele Ross wanted nothing at all to do with Christians or the church. In the most formative years of her life, the Christianity she experienced would have been enough to drive her anywhere but to the church.

The Ross family endured years of domestic turmoil resulting from her father's depressive illness. Subject to violent mood swings, he would shout, become violent and make chilling threats. Yet Eric Ross constantly searched for a God who would save him from his illness. For a short time he belonged to a small group of charismatic Christians whose prayer sessions for him took the form of renouncing the devil and commanding evil to depart from them. They would 'claim' healing for Eric, though Adele never saw any real change in her father's behaviour.

As these increasingly bizarre prayer sessions continued to produce no change in his behaviour, causes were sought further afield. First Eric and his friends decided that the household must be cleansed of evil. They then turned their prayer attention to Adele's mother, Serena, seeing her as the cause of the perceived uncleanness. When Serena refused to subject herself to processes she perceived as outlandish and accusatory, their suspicions of her deepened.

So growing up with a father suffering psychiatric illness was a painful time for Adele. The form of Christianity practised by her father compounded her pain as it attached blame to the family for causing his illness. Yet this was not enough to turn her off Christianity forever.

Eric and Serena Ross migrated to Australia from India in the 1970s. They were both Catholics, fourth or fifth generation adherents of that faith. They left New Delhi when Serena was 21 and Eric 30, wishing to begin a new lifestyle in Australia.

Their three daughters-Adele, Laura and Vanessa, now in their twenties and late teens-were born in the western suburbs of Sydney. The family moved to Canberra in 1985 when Adele was eight. Her only brother, Sandy, was born the year before. All of her parents' relatives still live in India.

Eric and Serena are both professional people. Eric is a teacher and Serena holds three degrees, two from an Indian and one from an Australian university. A training consultant for industrial and business personnel, she has worked in recent years with a large national institution in Canberra.

Like their parents, Adele and her sisters and brother were all baptised as Roman Catholics. Serena moved with the children to the Uniting Church in 1990, two years after her marriage finally collapsed.

Before the marriage break-up, Eric would take the family to catechism classes at the local Catholic church. Meeting in a classroom with several children, an adult from the church led them through lessons to prepare them for their First Holy Communion. Sometimes they worked through a booklet with the teacher, repeating the well-known prayers of the Catholic Church and answering questions.

Adele did not like the classroom situation and never completed the lessons. 'I just thought it was hypocrisy for my father to go there,' she recollects. 'When I look back, I can see it was more complicated than that but that's how it looked to me at the time. Actually, I blamed the whole church for it. My father's behaviour at home didn't give it a good advertisement and then the classes were very formal and put a lot of emphasis on learning facts—much like school, really.

'I also found the very formal prayers difficult to relate to, and I never could see the reason for telling a priest my confessions. But through it all, in spite of all these things, I always felt within that there was more to it than this, that there was something real, only I just wasn't seeing it. I wouldn't have said I was seeing much evidence of love around me. There was so much formality.'

Adele was 11 when her parents separated. Although Serena was no longer attending church, nor expressing any faith in a visible way, she had not deliberately abandoned her childhood belief in God. She felt the family situation made her children vulnerable. 'You see a lot of young people who seem to be lost and searching for meaning,' Serena says. 'They don't have a belief system. Maybe they go well for a while but then meet a crossroads and they have no spiritual support. So they make wrong choices. I didn't want my children to be like that. I was always worried that because I was on my own they were more vulnerable. If anything happened to me, what would become of them? There wouldn't be anyone around to give them spiritual or moral support.'

Adele remembers her early church attendance and says the family weren't just 'Sunday Christians'; they were 'one-hour Christians'. 'That's how long the services took. Then we'd come back home to Dad swearing and shouting. But, in the middle of all this, I had a kind of deeper peace. I can't explain it in any logical way, but I sort of believed that God was looking after us. Mum says she felt the same thing, even though she was worried that we had to depend on her and she didn't know if that was enough. Even now, I can look back on all the things that were hardest for us then and it isn't too upsetting to bring it back to mind.'

When she was 13, a close school friend named Beth experienced the death of her mother, who had suffered from cancer for 10 years. 'It was very sad,' Adele remembers, 'and hard for all the family and friends. But what mum especially noticed was that all her friends from the church were just wonderful to her. They used to call in and sit with her, and bring her flowers or food for the family. I guess she must have quietly compared that to what she was frightened of for us, with no kind of support base at all.'

Adele had been to some of the church's youth group activities with Beth and experienced similar warmth at first hand. 'What's more, Beth was right up front about her Christian faith. She had strong, clear views and she was always ready to discuss anything-evolution or abortion or whatever.'

In the same year that Beth's mother deteriorated in health, the whole Ross family went along to her church for the Christmas service, and the warmth of the experience ensured their continued attendance.

Some weeks later, they met a young woman called Bren, who was in charge of a dance group formed from members of the church. They danced at church events and gave stage performances expressing their Christian faith. The ages of those involved ranged from five to 18, mainly girls but not exclusively. The style of the dancing varied, depending on the ability of the children. Some dancers were experienced in ballet, gymnastics or other related fields, but most were local children having their first dance experience.

Bren was the major choreographer, who called upon the skills of the older children as circumstances dictated. Gradually, as she found ways of involving people, she handed over more and more tasks to group members, supervising their efforts. One day she approached Serena and she asked if one of her daughters could join the dance group. Serena was happy to oblige, and remembers replying: 'You can have them all, if you find they can dance.' Bren auditioned them and took all three daughters, and Sandy as well.

Adele found a mentor in Bren. Still in her early twenties and unmarried, Bren was an inspiring figure to a young girl. She got to know the group well and was loyal and committed to its members. Bren's dance ability and friendliness gave her credibility with her group of dancers. She demonstrated a clear and easily expressed Christian faith and Adele says she cared about each of the dancers' relationships with God.

Yet Bren was not an unusual product of her environment. She belonged to a church that generally supported people and she was a reflection of this culture. She encouraged the 40-odd members of her youth group to assist one another and in turn she received inspiration from them and from the general congregation, which numbered about three hundred people.

'My earliest understanding of God had a lot to do with rules and I was always anxious to keep them,' Adele says. 'Then we had this whole period of learning about the relationships of all these people in the Christian faith. When I was about 14, I went to a camp just outside Canberra. It was a standard enough camp as camps go, but it put its teaching focus on forgiveness and repentance. These were things about attitudes and states of mind-not rules-and suddenly a whole lot of things came together. The key speaker's messages made a real impact, about how we can have new life in Christ who died for us. Facts and stories of the past soon fitted real emotions, as the enormity of God's love for us hit home and the links became clear between Father, Son and Holy Spirit.

'There wasn't any particular meeting and no special occasion during the camp when anybody said anything I remember now, but I came away from it with clarity. It was the things that people showed in the way they related to each other and the things they said in ordinary dealings that really spoke to me. I suppose, with my background of so much tension in these areas, I was specially ready to be impressed.'

By then, all her family was at the Uniting Church. This made it fairly easy for Adele to join the next scheduled confirmation class. The church held such classes on a regular, repeating cycle and the next one was due six months after the camp, with half a dozen candidates. Adele joined it, although her decision to do so had been clearly made at the time of the camp.

In the few years after there were a variety of developments and changes at the church. The dance group disbanded as groups do with time, so the influence of that close-knit group was lost for Adele. It had been a major focus for her for three years, with one major tour each year and performances in shopping malls, outdoor parks and schools, often with Easter or Christmas emphases.

On the other hand, the Inter-School Christian Fellowship (ISCF) group at her local High School became important. With only half a dozen members, it was not highly visible but it did provide important encouragement both to her and the other Christians in her school years. It also gave her access to a range of healthy and enjoyable ISCF camps. Towards the end of her time at High School when she was 16 years old and in Year 10, she became a leader of her school ISCF group.

In her local school system, students moved to a senior school at the end of Year 10, for the final two years. Adele attended a nearby College where she became School Captain in Year 12. This committed her to a range of college activities and her involvement in ISCF became much more sporadic. The group itself was quite tiny with only two or three members and two guitar-playing teachers. In a co-educational college of 900 members this was indeed a low profile, though for those who were members, it remained as valuable as Adele's equivalent experience at High School.

Adele still lives in Canberra. Her faith continues to grow through a blend of ups and downs. One depressing down came about the time she left school, where a married Christian leader whom she respected made sexual advances toward her. She underwent all the classic symptoms of self-examination and guilt-'What was I wearing? Did I encourage him?'-and so on. The experience was potentially disillusioning for her, to say the least, but she is grateful for two things. The first was the teaching she had received at school about sexual harassment and how to deal with it. She had learned how to stay dignified, to state her case, clearly and unequivocally-'This is not making me feel good. Please go away.' This was effective in helping her bring the situation under control.

The other cause of her gratitude was the timing of the incident, which came just one day after she had made a new, personal pact with God. She had decided to follow him more deliberately and this decision helped her not to be overly bitter about the other person's betrayal.

More recently, Adele has attended a University group called Students for Christ, as well as her local church. The student group is about 15 strong and she is learning to see that the Christian faith is expressed in various ways and contexts, always by people with some weaknesses and failings. And the fact that some of these weaknesses and failings have played a dominant part in her life, without managing to obscure the love of God, she counts as evidence of just how strong that love is.

well, what made the difference?

1. Adele saw the care her friend's dying mother received from the church and it was important to her becoming open to God. What does this show about the potential of a collective witness, as the church conducts itself in love?

2. The acceptance Adele found among peers in the dance group and the commitment of her dance group leader cannot be overstated as influences upon her early moves to faith. What are the ways such experiences can be generated?

3. Regular church attendance built up Adele's on-going understanding of God. Do we always do all we can to attach young people to a church? What can we do about this?

4. At ISCF camp a number of factors about God clicked into place for Adele. Why are camps so often such strategic events for young people? What should they include to make them most valuable?

5. Adele's ISCF group gave her a place of fellowship and an avenue of service, even though it was not large. What can we learn from this?

daughter of an odd man out
Marija Skrinjaric

Laughter may well be the best medicine, but one can't help wondering over the profound dimensions of this human experience. For Marija Skrinjaric, it has been not only therapeutic, but part of a direct experience of the joy the Creator has in his children.

Once when she was 11 she visited her father, who was separated from her mother and who lived in the former Yugoslav city of Zagreb. They attended church and afterwards, Marija stayed the night at her father's place. 'That day in the church,' she remembers clearly, 'they had told us we could paint something, to make a church calendar-it was the start of the year. I drew the Tower of Babel and I had the picture in my pocket. I found it when I was going to bed.'

Marija's father, Nikola, had one of his friends from the church at home. When they came in to say goodnight to Marija, they looked at her picture. 'I've never been a great artist and they both said, "What is it?" My Dad asked me if it was some kind of cake. Then it was time for my prayers. Somehow what he had said came to mind and I started to laugh. But I'd never laughed like that before. It was a strong laugh and I couldn't stop. My Dad and his friend laughed too, but they didn't think it was that funny. Then, when they stopped laughing, I couldn't-I went on for 10 or 15 minutes. My Dad said it was the Holy Spirit's joy.'

For Marija, this experience transformed a young girl's faith. She not only 'felt really special in that time', she also encountered a deep, celebratory joy that only God can provide. And as her country entered its now infamous war, this experience was to be something very special to hang on to.

In Bregana, where Marija grew up, religious allegiances are clearly drawn-you are either a Catholic or an atheist. Which way you lean probably depends on whether you represent the area's older or newer traditions. Bregana is a village in what used to be called Yugoslavia. Today it is in Croatia, about 500 metres from the border with Slovenia. For generations, the people there have been raised in a formal and institutionalised sort of Catholicism. More recently in socialist times, a generation of atheists has been produced. Most people fit into one group or the other.

But Marija's father, Nikola, did not fit the mould of either. When Marija was a little girl, he experimented with a variety of beliefs. He had divorced from her mother, Ana, when Marija was three. Marija had stayed with her mother while her father lived elsewhere. Ana had no fixed religious views and Marija cannot remember hearing much about God during her early years.

'It was old Yugoslavia,' she says. 'We didn't have anything about God at school and I never heard anything from my mother. There was a bit from my grandparents and bits and pieces from some of my Catholic friends. Many of them went to the local church and I went sometimes too because of them. I got to know a little about God. I had the catechism and the Lord's Prayer and Ave Maria. I went to first communion. But no one really encouraged me to learn of God or to be religious, and I certainly didn't go to church every Sunday.

'But I got on well with my Dad, and I used to see him often. He has always had a big influence on my life. Till I was about eight, he tried all kinds of things. He had a Hare Krishna phase and he also was into Buddhism and Hinduism. It was as if he was searching for something he couldn't quite seem to find. I tried to do some of the things he did. He got interested in Bioenergy and over a period of time he became a healer. He learned from books and off another man he began to follow. He started to become a very successful healer. He used the Bioenergy techniques of herbal remedies and sweeping the hands over the patient's body to re-order the natural forces. He probably healed about 40,000 people in Croatia over a number of years.

'He became very popular, as you could understand-everyone wanted him to heal them. But he kept questioning and he noticed that all these people that he healed just got sick again with something else some time later. The healing was just temporary. He had great power, was making a lot of money and of course, was very popular. But he wasn't settled in it.

'Maybe that's why he went with some friends one day to the Catholic church. I don't know how they got him to go, but he did, and as a consequence he started to read the Bible. He even put away his Bioenergy things for a while, but after some time he came back to them again and got back all his old powers, and he forgot the Bible. But he'd had a taste and maybe God hadn't forgotten him. He still wasn't restful in himself. After a year or two, someone took him to a Protestant church in Zagreb.'

Zagreb is the capital of Croatia, with a population of just over a million. It lies 28 kilometres east of Bregana and is more cosmopolitan and less traditional in outlook than a small village like Bregana. Among the two or three thousand inhabitants of Bregana, you are unlikely to meet anyone who is not a Catholic, while in Zagreb, you might come across small groups of people belonging to other Christian denominations, as well as sects and cults. But everything is under the shadow of the Roman Catholic church.

Marija's father, Nikola, was taken to the Good News Church, called Severinska by its members, after the street where it is situated. He said later that that day was 'his day'. He didn't say what the message was about. But he did say that he heard God's message for him. He said he got all the answers to his questions about life and about God. That day he accepted Christ and he became a man with a changed direction.

Marija was eight years old at the time. She continued to live alone with her mother, with visits to her father. But even in those circumstances, she could see there were changes. 'He was kind of different,' she remembers. 'He was more settled and at peace. He even tried to be reconciled to Mum, but she didn't want that. He gave me some Christian books, although they didn't mean much to me at the time. But he didn't do anything about Bioenergy any more and he had given up chasing other religions.'

Nikola continued to cast around for his niche within the Christian faith. A year or two later, when Marija was ten, he took her to a service at Christ's Pentecostal Church in Zagreb, a classic Pentecostal service. Marija had never imagined anything like it, and she was not impressed.

'It was weird for me. It was only a few weeks after my first communion, at the very formal Catholic church in Bregana. Here, at this bizarre church in Zagreb, there were all sorts of things going on. Some people were crying and some were laughing, some of them were talking in languages I'd never heard before, half of them had their arms in the air-it was just weird. The contrast to the church I had gone to in Bregana was total. I don't even remember what I thought about God in the middle of it all.'

Marija was scared, but also angry with her father for taking her there. When they arrived home, she told him she didn't want to go there any more.

During the summer of that year, she went to the Adriatic island of Krk with her father. They stayed with Stanko Jambrek, the pastor of the Good News Church in Zagreb, his wife Ljubinka and another lady. Marija got on well with Ljubinka, an attractive person who was gentle and good with children. So, when Nikola asked Marija to come to their church, a couple of weeks after they returned from the coast, she said yes. She remembers, that they thought she could help Ljubinka with the children in the Sunday school.

In reality, it wasn't that easy. Marija's father lived in Zagreb, where the church was, and Marija lived in Bregana. Although not too far away, it required two buses to get to Zagreb. Halfway there, Marija realised she didn't know exactly where to go.

'My Dad told me it was in Tresnjevka. I knew where that was. It's a suburb of Zagreb. He told me that the services were at 10 o'clock every Sunday, and I said that was all right too. That was about the start of the week. But my Dad hadn't called me in the meantime. Anyway, I got onto the bus at Bregana and I had to change buses at Samobor. Samobor is a market town, between Zagreb and Bregana.

'So I got off the bus at Samobor and, while I was waiting for the second bus, I saw someone who looked familiar. When I looked at him again, it was my Dad! So I went over to him, and he said, "What on earth are you doing here?" I replied, "I'm going to church with you." He was pleased about this, but also surprised. He asked me how I found him and I hadn't thought about it. But when I look back, I wonder why I was there. I didn't know where I was going-not the street or anywhere, just the suburb, and I bumped into him without either of us planning for it.'

Marija's only church experiences to this stage were the extreme Pentecostal incident that had alarmed her a few months before, and the formal Catholic churches of her friends at school. When she arrived with her father at the church belonging to the pastor she had already met, she automatically expected the traditional expression of Catholic worship.

'I crossed myself as I went in, as the people did in the churches around Bregana, but looking around me at the other people, I saw no one else did that. I was very embarrassed, but no one seemed to mind and the service began. It was very peaceful. They sang nice songs. It was better than that other Pentecostal Church. I liked the people because they liked me. I went to the Sunday school that day, with Ljubinka and all the other children and I felt accepted there.

'I went back to the church on other Sundays, and began to really enjoy the worship time and the singing. At first, I was just listening to the music, but after a while I became aware of the words and I started to think about them. Even though I was going to the Sunday school, and so never heard a sermon, I began to think about the words the people were singing.

'After a few months, I stopped going to the Sunday school because I wanted to stay in the service and listen to the sermon. I don't know if you'd expect a 10 year old child to respond to what was going on in the church service, but I did. I felt so many times God's presence, whispering in my ear that he loved me. That was the biggest thing that influenced my acceptance in my heart.'

Marija was 11 when she was baptised. She is among the youngest ever to be baptised at the Good News Church. Usually, the practice is to wait until the candidate is 13 or 14, or even older.

'My Dad understood me. Stanko and others did too. They took me seriously and they were willing to baptise me. I remember that day well-17 October 1990. I came to the water and they were asking me questions so I could state my faith, and I have clear mental pictures of the faces of the people in the church, while I was answering. I was baptised with three other people, who were all 19 or 20.

'I don't know how my Mum felt about this baptising-she didn't come to it-but she did tell me one time that I was too grown up for my age. I was trying to tell her about Jesus and how he loves her too, but she didn't understand me and she said, "Well, you're too young for all of this." It was all quite foreign to her.

'I'm glad I met God early. Knowing him doesn't turn life into a fairy story, but I am so thankful that I have been able to keep out of a lot of bad things people often meet in their teenage years. Many of those people I know, who became Christians when they were 18 or 19, are sorry because of the things they have done in their past. I'm glad that I didn't go through a lot of those things.

'It was hard for me in other ways, of course. Life is not all perfect for anyone. My Dad was very helpful to me, and Miki and Nada Jonke were, too. They were also in the church. But often they weren't with me. They were in Zagreb and I was in Bregana with my mother. I didn't know one other Christian in Bregana, and Zagreb is an hour and a half away.

Marija never missed a Sunday at church for the next year, except once when she was in hospital. But then the war started. The war meant a lot of different things, of course, to the people of the former Yugoslavia. For Marija, as a 12 year old, it made its biggest personal impression when her father went to Bosnia. 'He didn't have to go. It's nearly 500 kilometres from Zagreb to Sarajevo, and another three hundred to Mostar, which is where he went. But he felt he had to go and do humanitarian work, and then God called him to stay and do missionary work. It was the worst time of the war, and people where I lived, up near Slovenia, said he must be crazy. It was relatively safe around Zagreb, but in Mostar there were bombs and snipers, and a lot of shooting.

'People asked me if I was afraid for him, and of course I missed him and I wanted him here, but really I wasn't fearful for him. I don't know why-I guess God gave me this peace. When I started to see what he was doing there, I just knew it was right. He's still there. He has a church there with 200 or more people and he's started a second one. There's a church in east Mostar and one in west-it's a divided city-and six or seven Protestant churches in Bosnia. It's an amazing story all by itself.

'But for me, at the time, it meant I was home on my own with my Mum, and all our friends were not Christians. My mother got a new husband around that time and it was hard for me to communicate with him. I went to church still, but it got to be erratic and then quite rare. There were also some problems in the Good News Church and it wasn't easy. The church went in three different directions, with three different leaders. I wanted to go with Miki Jonke, who had always been friendly with my Dad, and me but he ended up at Agape Church in Dubrava, two and a half hours from my place. It's in the western suburbs of Zagreb, maybe 50 kilometres away, and it was too far, especially in the evenings. Suddenly, the people I had grown up with in my Christian faith were all gone-to Bosnia, to another church, and the Jambreks had gone to America.'

In Christian terms, Marija spent the next few years discouraged, wondering how she would manage. She stopped going to church. At 14, she started at Anton Gustav Matos Gymnasium, Croatia's equivalent of a grammar school. There she made a number of new friends, none of them Christian, as she didn't know any Christians there. Her choice of friends perhaps helped her frame of reference move further from God and she began to place less emphasis on the Bible. She knew what was happening; what she didn't know was how to stop it. But she found a lifeline in a number of teenage camps and conferences she was able to attend. There she met Christians from all over Croatia.

In the summer of her first year at high school she went to Crikvenica, on the Adriatic coast, where a team was helping to build the Christian Life Centre. Her father had brought some people up from Mostar, so she was not entirely without Christian links, although these were scattered and sporadic.

This phase lasted for two or three years. She finished the second grade in High School, still torn between her faith and her friends. She still prayed and she knew that God helped her at school. She often saw evidence of that, mostly in little things, but she found it hard to relate to God. Near the end of second year, while visiting her father in Mostar, she met an American missionary friend of his.

'I told him I was searching for Christian friends, but I didn't know anyone. I was thrilled when he told me that he had a team from America who were coming to Zagreb to do a summer mission and that I might be able to join them. It sounded terrific, but then I found out they would be there ten days before I was going to finish school and I would need special permission to end school early and go with them. I didn't see how anyone would think this was a good cause for me to join, but I really prayed about it-and I got permission.

'But it still wasn't over. It must have been a trial of my faith. With everything in place and all ready to go, there was a bombing of Zagreb and the US Government refused to let the team come to Croatia. There were 27 of them and the American authorities thought it would be too much of a risk.

'But this team was all prepared and they didn't want to stay at home. Instead, they organised to go to Slovenia. Slovenia! Even closer to me! Bregana is right on the border. It was like this team was coming right to where I was. We went to boot camp in Zenavlje.'

Zenavlje is a rural Slovenian village, about 100 kilometres from

Bregana. 'Boot camp' is a term borrowed from the American military, meaning a preparation time. At a little church in Zenavlje the team, with Marija, spent some days in teaching, singing, fellowship and training, and in personal spiritual development. To Marija, it was the end of a desert. 'I realised how far I had slipped in four years and I said, "It has to stop." I wept before God and he released me. I imagined my heart full of thorns and rubbish, and as I prayed and wept, it disappeared. I promised myself and God that I would not let this happen again. We had a three week mission in Slovenia and we were all like one big family on the team. I went home stronger and also scared to be back on my own. Yet I believed that God would connect me up with his family again.

'I went on a few more camps that summer, sort of feeding my batteries for another year. Then I went back to school, to start the third grade. It wasn't like I thought it would be in the summer. There was still no church. I was praying all the time that God would send at least one person to be near me.

'Well, the school year started and nothing seemed to be very different. But we had a young teacher for our English class, maybe 25 years old. She asked our class to deliver a kind of speech on what we had been doing over the holidays. We were to take it in turns and she asked me first, because she knew I had been with the Americans, and I suppose she thought it would be different and interesting.

'So I told the class everything we had done. I told them how we had shared about Jesus and everything. I was glad about this, because before that I had never made any open kind of statement of my faith. Some of them knew, of course, but it hadn't been that open. I got to the end of my talk, and when I'd finished, my teacher said to me, "Do you know Narcissa?" "No," I said, "Who's Narcissa?" "I'll tell you about it later," she said, "after class. It sounds like you might like to meet Narcissa and her husband."

'I was very excited about this, and wondered who they could be. Perhaps they were missionaries? I talked to my Dad and he said, "Be careful. They might be Mormons or something." And I prayed, "Oh God, please let them be real, good Christians." '

Narcissa and Joe Saladino turned out to be just that. They were an American couple who had moved to the area for business reasons three years before. Marija's English teacher met one of their daughters and told Marija that they held Bible studies in their home. This answered her prayers for Christian fellowship. The Saladinos lived in Samobor, right next to Marija's home village of Bregana, five minutes away by bus.

She was thrilled. Initially, she didn't know whether they were real Christians or not, but she did know that she wanted to go and find out. She talked to Narcissa on the phone and was told that the group met on Saturday. Narcissa invited her to join them. When she went the next weekend, she found 10 young people present. 'It was like church!' Marija says. 'Even though we sat in a house, in a circle, on ordinary chairs-it was real! We sang and we had a sermon, and I liked it. They asked me who I was and I said I'd been praying for this to happen for the last six years. They were all amazed. It gave us all new hope. In Slovenia, God had given me a sign that he would never leave me. Now he'd given me a whole group!'

In the May and June of 1996, Marija made a visit to Atlanta in the USA, a kind of reciprocal visit for the American team who had come to Slovenia. She went with 16 others from the Balkan states. 'Listen to what they were,' she says. 'Slovenia, Bosnia, Serbia, Croatia, Bulgaria. No one could believe that these nations, still technically in a war zone, could come together in the same place and worship the same God.'

The group in Samobor is quietly growing. There are 30 regular attenders and some others who come intermittently. Most are young and many are students. Marija herself, now in her early twenties, completed her high schooling in 1997. Meanwhile, she has had the opportunity to serve God in a local house group. Joe and Narcissa have no long-term visas to remain in the area and every three months the fellowship faces the possibility of losing them.

Some members of the group are developing preaching and teaching abilities; some are leading Bible studies. Marija leads the drama group. She would like to study drama in the US, then return home and use those skills in Christian service in Croatia. She also leads some of the worship and is able to help the group as a translator. There are services in both English and Croatian. She pauses for a charitably long time before acknowledging that Joe and Narcissa's Croatian is 'hopeless'.

It's as well the group is not totally reliant on the Saladinos, for even if they become fluent in the language, they might move. Clearly, the area needs its Marijas and others like her. God seems to be locating them.

well, what made the difference?

1. Marija obviously grasped deep Christian concepts at an early age despite lack of Christian teaching. How important is it to know where young people's understanding is at before we develop programs and courses for them? Or will those who are keen like Marija simply stand out?

2. The first church she attended scared her and made her angry with her father. When should worship take into account how other people, children in particular, might perceive it? How can we give young people authentic worship experiences?

come back after assembly

Emily Mitchell

When Emily Mitchell first asked her parents if she could attend church with friends she had made during camp, she could not have predicted the response. After all, before the family moved to Canberra, they had attended their local Catholic church in Melbourne. So, they would probably be excited, right? Well, not quite. Emily's parents forbade her from attending the Reformed church in Rivett, a few suburbs away. They wouldn't even give a reason. 'They just said, "No, you can't," ' Emily recalls. 'I was surprised and hurt. I didn't understand it.'

On a sunny afternoon at the Australian National University, Emily, in her second year studying commerce, remembered her first year as a Christian. 'What I'd really like to do after Uni, is youth camping work,' she says. 'But the study won't do me any harm and the degree will be useful as well.' A tall, athletic looking girl with broad shoulders and a tanned skin, she has a relaxed manner. There's an alertness about her that would fit well with camping work.

Emily is in her early twenties, with two younger sisters, Angela and Rozlyn. Her father is an accountant with the Department of Administrative Services and her mother an administrative assistant at ANU. The family has lived in Canberra since Emily was seven.

They moved to Canberra temporarily for her father's work, which expanded soon after the shift. 'I went to a Catholic school in Melbourne,' she says. 'My family were regular attenders at the church the school was attached to. When we came to Canberra, they enrolled me in a state primary school because we weren't going to be here long and it was close to our home. But the job grew and it seemed unnecessary to shift me from the school, so I finished my primary schooling in the state system.

'The family loosened its church ties at the same time, as a reaction to circumstance. They had no immediate church friends in Canberra and when they thought they'd only be here a short time they didn't seem to really make an effort to get into another church. By the time they found they were staying on, they had a pattern established.'

Effectively, she had no real Christian teaching until she was 14, in Year 9 at Stromlo High School in her local area of Weston Creek. When it did re-enter her life, it came in a haphazard fashion. In Canberra, a non-denominational voluntary group called Youth Adventure Holidays runs camps for young people, assisted by government funding. A woman came to Stromlo High to advertise these camps.

'She came to a full assembly-maybe six or seven hundred pupils there. She did her pitch and it sounded all right, and she said we could see her after assembly to get some brochures if we were interested. I said to my friend, "Let's go and get a brochure." She said, "Really? What for? Do you want to go to this camp?" "I don't know," I said. "But it's Maths next lesson. If we go and get a brochure, we'll be late for it. Come on!"

'So we went and got the brochure. We were late for Maths. But then we got looking at the brochure and we thought we'd go to the camp. It looked good-up by the Murrumbidgee, half an hour out of town, and they put on a bus. Six days in tents sounded good.'

The Murrumbidgee River is part of the Murray-Darling waterway that drains the area west of the Snowy Mountains and much of the south-eastern corner of Australia. North of Canberra, the river flows through rocky country, the domain of magpies and crows. There is an impression of space. The soil is red and gritty, with a harshness that is stark and grand. Set in this terrain is the campsite, a little more cultivated than the bush. It consists of a paddock on a farm right next to the river, a shed, a small kitchen and space for tents.

There is a rich variety of bird life-grey and pink galahs, raucous herds of sulphur-crested cockatoos and rainbow lorikeets. Lorikeets have purple and red and green and blue and yellow feathers and are extravagantly riotous in colour. But their colouring is so cleverly fashioned that you could step on one in the grass if the bird didn't choose to move. As well there are kookaburras with a call like a staccato siren and a beak like a broad sword, and tiny little flittering birds that give the appearance of airborne mice. Ants as long as your finger nail with bulbous backsides counterbalance the enormous loads they carry-the rugby forwards of the ant kingdom. There are various wild flowers, tiny and delicate, and kangaroos that lope past like people running on a moving walkway.

Youth Adventure Holidays wanted young people to experience more than that. Along with the magnificence of creation, they also wanted to point towards the person of the Creator. They spread their advertising wide and took campers from wherever they found them. The advertising included a special pitch towards families who might find it financially difficult to send their children camping. And they made sure their leaders were all Christians and expected them to put their faith on show.

Emily's school friend pulled out of the camp and she ended up going on her own. Though she was the only one from her school who went, it didn't bother her. 'We had these adventure activities during the day,' she recalls. 'Abseiling and caving and things like that-most of them were new to me. We did them in small groups of six or seven campers and a couple of leaders.

Then we had a CD time every evening. It stands for Christian Discovery. A different leader each evening spoke for half an hour on some Bible story or life theme straight before we went to bed. Then we'd head off in our tent groups and discuss the theme for the night in our smaller groups before we went to sleep. It was good. A lot of us hadn't ever talked about these things before.'

The camp comprised about 25 campers and over a dozen leaders who were in their late teens and early 20s, a balance that provided for close, mentoring relationships. 'They were great leaders-really fun to be with,' Emily says. 'They were so good to each other and to the campers. It made you really respect them. They were often silly and made you laugh, but they had something I didn't. I'm generally a fairly happy person but they had a different joy. There seemed a sort of depth to it.'

Emily didn't just find the lives of the leaders challenging; they were also up-front about their faith in a relaxed but intelligent way. On one night in the discussion time, Emily's tent leader asked her a question. It wasn't anything very deep, just something factual from the Bible. But it niggled away at Emily, because she was sure she knew the answer. 'I think I must have remembered it from the Catholic school in Melbourne. Whatever it was, I knew it, and I was very surprised. I felt that maybe there was more to these little chats than I had realised. I tuned in a lot more after that and I really watched the leaders. Now, I was interested.

'My tent leader's question was important to me, yet I have never had any contact with her since that camp. She was an exchange student from the United States who returned never knowing the spark she left in me. But I did make some good friends on the camp and I felt really close to them. We went home at the end of the week and I was really, really flat. I missed the leaders and campers a lot, and it was back to the usual old things.'

A couple of days after the camp, Emily started looking at a Gideon Bible she'd been given in Year 7, her first year at high school. She received the Bible when the Gideons visited Stromlo High School giving one to all the first year students. Emily hadn't looked at the Bible in the two and a half years since receiving it. The only other Bible she knew of was a very old version belonging to her mother.

'After the camp, in that flat period, I looked through my Gideon Bible and I prayed the prayer at the back of it for when you want to become a Christian. There was a place where you could sign your name and put in the date. I did that too. I didn't have much understanding about it but I knew I wanted to be in, whatever it was.'

In the weeks following the camp, Emily had a number of contacts with campers. Some of the leaders gave her a phone call, there were some reunions and she was invited to a youth group with some of the girls at the Reformed Church in Rivett, a neighbouring suburb. The youth group was a Friday night affair and her parents had no objections to her attending it reasonably regularly until the end of the year.

At Easter the following year, in 1993, Emily was off again to the Youth Adventure Camp at the same site. Her faith was still at the fledgling stage and she thinks it had not yet begun to produce visible changes in her living patterns. This time her cabin leader was a student teacher named Katie de Veau, from the University of Canberra. She provided an inspiring role model, was friendly and interested in her campers.

The friendship with Katie came at a very important time in Emily's Christian development. 'I learned heaps from her,' she says. 'She's married now but she's stayed in touch. Katie's just been so natural and friendly-we've discussed all sorts of things. I could ask her anything and have often turned to her for answers about the whole Christian thing. She attends a Baptist Church. Although she's five years older than I am, I have always felt really comfortable around her.'

In the months after this second camp, Emily attended a weekend camp or two and felt a growing sense of belonging to the group at large and went back to the Rivett youth group on Friday night. But when she first asked if she could attend church there on Sunday, her parents suddenly refused. 'They encouraged me to go to the various camps and were pleased enough for me to go to the youth group. I think they didn't know very much about the Reformed church, which was obviously quite different from churches they had known. They feared some kind of cult. So they wouldn't let me go.'

Katie proved to be a wise and faithful friend during this time. 'I asked her a lot of questions and learned heaps from her,' Emily remembers. 'I would always turn to her when I was upset or confused about my parents. I slept over at her house a few times but before that, she came to dinner at my place and met my parents properly. It was good, because it helped them not to worry so much about the sort of person she was or what she might be doing. I could always turn up at her house whenever I needed to and she would always have time for me. I don't see her so much these days, but I still know that if I needed to talk to her, she would find the time. She is one of those incredibly loving people who you can't help but like the first time you meet them. She showed me Christ, and I love her heaps.'

In September that year, Emily was off to camp again but this time as a leader. She co-led a group with Katie de Veau for year 5 and 6 primary school children-nine and ten year olds, at Attunga, a site half way between Canberra and Sydney.

After finishing Year 10, she moved to a senior school to complete Years 11 and 12 as is the practice in Canberra. While most of her friends went to another college, she chose Phillip College in the neighbouring district of the Woden Valley. About half way through Year 11, since the Rivett Reform group stopped after Year 10, she began attending a youth group at Weston Creek Uniting Church at the invitation of a friend from Stromlo.

'We started an ISCF group at Phillip College,' Emily says. 'There had been one at the College in years gone by but it had lapsed. We knew about ISCF from Stromlo, though I hadn't gone to it there until just before I left. There were a couple of Stromlo girls with me at Phillip and half a dozen of us started a group, which grew to about a dozen. Some of the guys later joined it, too. We kept that on through the two years, mostly running it ourselves. It wasn't too brilliant and didn't seem to achieve much but it gave us a focus and helped develop the friendships. It gave us a place where we could talk about God. I still wasn't allowed to go to church through a lot of this time, so talking to people was quite important to me. Sometimes people came in and spoke to our group-Phil Lindsay, the Capital Territory Scripture Union worker was one of these. Everything helps, and for me it was ISCF and the youth group in my last years at college, and my Christian friends.'

That last year at College, Emily's parents allowed her to start attending church. 'It happened quite suddenly,' she says. 'I wasn't really expecting it. I was going to the Weston Creek Uniting youth group on Sunday afternoons and on Saturday nights. Most of my friends stayed on for church after the Bible study sessions while I went home. Every now and then I'd test the situation again-"Why can't I go to church?" and so on. We argued about it but then one Sunday, around Easter of my first year at Uni, my mother suddenly said, "Yes, you can." I looked at her-you know, Have I got this right?-then took off.

I've been going ever since, and my parents have been good about it.'

Emily's sister Angela is a Christian now, too. She has been on some of the Youth Adventure Holiday camps and used to talk to Emily about it a lot when she started going. 'She came to youth group with me and now she goes to Weston Creek Uniting. We go together-Mum lends us her car. Angela's story is much like mine, just a year or two behind. She's got her own circle of friends at the youth group and her own faith. Rozlyn's been on a couple of camps too.'

Emily keeps going back to the camps as a leader, in September, at Easter and also in July. In October of 1996, Emily had her first taste as camp director. She's grateful for the opportunity, describing the experience as exciting though also hard, especially when the discipline of campers came up as an issue.

Now in her early 20s, Emily has started well on her Christian journey, travelling steadily down it. Her wish to one day be a camps youth worker is being tested already and she has still some hours to log in toward the necessary experience.

It's a long way from the time she picked up a camp brochure from a visitor to school assembly, just so she could stay out of a Maths class a little bit longer. Sitting under a tree in Canberra, reflecting on the key steps to her development to a Christian faith, she says, 'It's funny what little things can lead on to a great effect. It's a bit scary, really.'

well, what made the difference?

1. The discovery that she knew something of what the camp leaders were talking about was very influential for Emily. Why is teaching which is based on what a person already

knows, rather than on what they do not know, often very powerful?

2. The leaders at the camp, especially Katie de Veau, had a big impact. Elsewhere in this book, people speak often of the profound influence of camp leaders. How big a factor in all this is the sense that many turned up at camps expecting Christians to be weird, only to discover that they were normal, well-balanced people?

3. Emily committed her life to God after reading the Bible given to her, years before, by the Gideons. The prayer at the back of the Bible gave her a form for a commitment when she was by herself. How can we provide forms such as this for turning interest into action?

4. Katie de Veau was for some time a very special friend to Emily, even after she was married. How important or possible is it to maintain such friendships as circumstances change? How can we provide replacements?

patched, healed and growing

John Langham

It might seem strange that one of the significant events in John Langham's Christian experience happened over a bowl of breakfast cereal when he was ten. Nevertheless, when he sat down that day to breakfast with his mother Jane, it wasn't just the fabric of his morning routine that was transformed.

In his early childhood, John exhibited a severe allergy to wheat products, lactose, artificial colouring and caffeine. His strict dietary regime excluded milk, caffeine, Coca-Cola and anything containing wheat flour; which, when you think about it, excluded much of what most people take for granted for breakfast or almost any other meal.

One day his mother took him to visit a priest in Wellington, New Zealand, who had a ministry of healing through prayer. 'We went in to see him and he talked with us for a while,' John recalls. 'I can't remember all the details, but it boiled down to, "If you have faith, you can be healed." We only made the one visit to the priest, but it lasted the best part of an afternoon. We talked about the whole issue quite a lot, and then he prayed for me and asked for the allergies to be removed.'

John's memories are now vague. The visit was unhurried but not overlong. His mother was present throughout the proceedings. Nothing dramatic happened and he cannot remember any special effects being created by the prayer or in conjunction with it. They talked, prayed and left, and in the process received the central message, 'If you have faith, you can be healed.'

'So the next day, we tried some wheat for breakfast,' John recalls. 'I don't remember any special anxiety surrounding the breakfast. I didn't feel any and Mum never suggested it. She had a lot of faith and completely trusted the Lord would heal me.'

There was no hyperactive reaction-he ate what was put in front of him and showed no ill effects. His mother had a lot on the line, for she was concerned not only about her oldest son's physical health but also for his faith-would he be encouraged or daunted by the outcome?

John cannot recall her showing any apprehension. What he can remember is her 'strong faith' and that through this event he came to know that God was alive and real. 'I knew, from then on, that God was active. I didn't need anyone to convince me.'

Jane's memory has a slightly different emphasis. 'The significant thing for me is the healing of memories that Father Rea prayed for at the time. It seems to have worked for John too-he has such a lack of memory of the difficult past, which had really been very hard. I also remember Father Rea's words at the end of the prayer time, when he said to us, "God will act. He always answers prayer. Either you will be healed, or you will be given grace to cope with your allergies. I don't know which it will be, but God will show you very soon."

The first test was actually on the way home, when we called in to see a friend who offered us a fresh pikelet, and I thought, "This must be it." The breakfast was the next day, and John was fine through both these times. And yes, I did feel my faith was on the line. How can you not feel, "What if nothing happens?" If John remembers "my strong faith" out of all of this, then that's just another mark of the goodness of God.'

While John's faith was significantly affected by the healing of his allergies, his choice of career has been influenced by other medical problems. A very competitive runner and rugby player,

John received his fair share of injuries, spending a lot of time with doctors. 'I developed a plica in my knee from running too much-that's a fold of a membrane caught between the bones. I was in the sixth form, training for the national cross-country championship race. It put me out.' Over the years he has hurt himself playing rugby, and along with this there has been a twisted ankle, a dislocated collarbone and a damaged rotator cuff muscle in his shoulder. Through numerous visits to the doctor for these injuries, John became interested in his various treatments. 'They did some X-rays and talked about muscles and things, and I got interested in checking through books on the background to it. When I was leaving college, I wanted to be challenged and useful, so I applied for med. school and they took me in.'

Born in Southampton, England, John moved to New Zealand with his family when he was eight because his father was pursuing a job opportunity with a shipping company. John didn't want to go. 'I was just about to move to the top deck of the school bus,' he explains, 'where you only got to after you'd stopped being among the little kids. Then my family moved! I never did get there.'

On arrival in the new country, he was forcefully reminded that he was a stranger. 'I went to St Francis Xavier Catholic school in Tawa, near Wellington, and they called me a Pom for two years. They didn't get over it till I went on to Tawa Intermediate.' John moved to Tawa Intermediate after his three years at Francis Xavier, spending two years there before going on to Tawa College.

The family were members of the parish of Our Lady of Fatima Catholic Church in Tawa. John received his early Christian education there and prior to that, at primary school in Southampton. 'We had Religious Education at school and we went to services pretty regularly. It was always a part of our life-no big deal, just an expected feature. We used to work from these brightly coloured RE sheets a few times a week, mostly working on a story from the Bible. As I remember them now, they were mostly narrative and history, rather than any kind of applied teaching for life. It was a sort of Sunday school style, where you worked with a teacher and filled out the sheets. We never gave it any special kind of attention-it was just part of school, really.'

He attended mass with the school on the first Friday of every month. 'Each class took it in turns to organise it and the priest came along to do his thing,' he recalls. 'We always used to enjoy the actual process and the event. Compared with Sunday mass at church, it was a fun occasion, since we never had any children's liturgy or special program at church.'

A year or two after the family arrived in Tawa, Jane Langham helped organise a children's program for the church. Jane was enthusiastic about the expansion of children's education there and had always been keen to see her own children receive a Christian education. She often read to them from the Bible or from books on the saints.

John recalls this aspect of his Christian education as having a factual or historical basis. But as a result of the healing of his allergies through the priest's prayers, these facts transformed into events and the history began to become significant to him.

When he moved from the Catholic education system to Tawa Intermediate, a state school, no RE program was offered there. But as a children's liturgy began at his church so this lessened the effect of the change.

The next significant development in John's Christian understanding came two years later when he was 13. The Catholic-run New Zealand Redwood Centre held annual summer camps in the Christmas holidays. John attended at a week-long camp at Paraparaumu, just out of Wellington during the summer holidays. The leaders were Andy and Anne Lovell. Their desire was to teach the gospel in congenial surroundings with an emphasis on personal experience and sharing. 'There was a new focus on reading the Bible in a personal way. The actual activities were fairly standard camp stuff. But the leaders were very important to us-people a few years older than us, who were into life and modelled a bit of glamour, while demonstrating a genuine Christian faith of their own.'

Along with the youth leaders there were some strategically placed adults in the camping program, with the Lovells acting as camp parents. 'I went and had a bit of a talk to them,' John commented, 'and there was a priest in attendance who was available to hear confessions. One of the evenings was given over to a reconciliation service.'

The leaders came from all over Wellington. The Lovells selected them for their ability to do what John Langham observed them doing-living a viable and vigorous faith. Many had been involved in a charismatic Catholic youth rally, the Firepower Rally, which held weekend gatherings around the Wellington area.

For John, the chief value of the camp was that God began to become more personal. Although he believed in a God who was real, God had always seemed to be part of a religious process. Unexpectedly, the Firepower people brought God into range.

During John's next year at school, fourth form or Year 9, he joined the Tawa College Inter School Christian Fellowship (ISCF) group, under the guidance of his older sister, Rachel. She too had experienced the camp and Firepower Rally and was keen to see John benefit from something similar. Two additional important experiences came about over the next couple of years. Over 30 people from all sorts of different church backgrounds were attracted to the ISCF group at meetings at Tawa College. 'My Catholic background had been strong on routines in worship, and this was positive in many ways. Some of the others came from a strong tradition of Bible study. These things got mixed in and shared around in discussion groups. The really good thing about ISCF was this rich mixing of different emphases-you got a chance to see what other people were doing. At the same time, you were testing your own ideas. I hadn't done much of this before. It was really helpful to talk about your faith and to hear other people talking about theirs. As well, you got to know a few people around the school. It was good to know that the seniors were keeping an eye out for the third formers.'

In this way, John describes how he grew into an assured Christian faith that was focused not so much on a point, but on a process. Cardinal Tom Williams, the Catholic Bishop of Wellington, remarks that this is a deliberate aim of the church. 'We don't regard the Damascus Road as the norm,' he said. 'Our emphasis is on steady teaching, and we expect people to grow in understanding and commitment.'

Certainly this is John Langham's testimony. 'Of course, there were significant events along the way,' John recalls. 'For some of my friends from other traditions, baptism was one of those events, a mature confession of faith. For me, as I had been baptised as an infant, my equivalent was confirmation when we had a series of about eight evening sessions on the nature of the faith, ending with a public statement of confirmation. Quite a few of us completed the course. It didn't mean much to some of them, I don't think. My year group had undergone all the sacraments together, so when it was time for confirmation we were all contacted-it was just what you do at 15. But to me, it was very significant. This was my time to put a conscious hand on all the growing that had been going on and to become quite deliberate about the continuing development. My confirmation came at just the right time. It was stand and be counted time.'

In his last couple of years at school John helped lead the ISCF. He also ran a youth group in a neighbouring church and a youth discussion group at his own. John is now well into studying towards his medical degree at Auckland University and is enjoying the course. He still runs a bit for recreation and plays the odd social rugby match as a full back. When he moved to Auckland in 1997, he shifted his church allegiance, becoming a part of Eden Chapel. 'I was looking for a pattern of teaching in the sermon times,' John says. 'Eden Chapel is strong on that and I've gone to Titahi Bay Chapel in Wellington when I've been home, for the same reason. My mother would have preferred me to have stayed in a Catholic Church but, basically, she's glad to know the reality's still there.'

The 'reality' in John's life has become a transforming presence-not a static, unchanging belief, but the presence of the Holy Spirit, who brings together different experiences and beliefs into a unique relationship with God. John could hardly have imagined on that morning over a decade earlier, that not only would he be able to eat a normal breakfast, but that being able to do so would become a major factor in knowing personally, the God he had previously only known about.

well, what made the difference?

1. When John's mother took an active interest in his spiritual welfare she may or may not have been able to help make these truths more personal. Is it any more difficult for a parent to make personal the facts about the Christian life? Are there things that a parent can do that a church leader can't, and vice versa?

2. John's experience of healing was quite miraculous. If he hadn't been healed, how might he have viewed the church if he had suffered an allergic reaction to his breakfast immediately following the priest's prayers for his healing? What tension is there between praying bold prayers that may not be answered literally. How would you counsel a disillusioned person?

3. The stimulus of an inter-denominational group of peers who showed him different approaches to the Christian life was significant for John. How important is it to be around Christians of varying traditions to allow our understanding of faith to be refined in this way? How can we facilitate that for the young people we know?

by various pathways

There is no simple mix of ingredients to which we can merely add water then stir, to see a conversion. However, these stories are helpful in re-examining the role we might play in the drama of faith.

Many mysteries are revealed in the course of these fourteen stories, provoking serious questions. Why, for instance, did Annette Bailey and Tarsh Koia find such a pull towards Christianity given the limited Christian teaching they received as children? What gave Graham Eagle the power to follow a Christian faith when all his home influences were in stark contrast to it? When did Rene Galbes' rebellious questions give way to listening for answers? Why didn't Wayne Dixon abandon a God who was not strong enough to hold his parents together or Gina Wong find in the cold light of day that her decision for Jesus the night before had been a figment of her mind?

And why didn't Ron Tevita let his brother Manu attend his Bible studies on his own? What kept Adele Ross from abandoning faith when she felt let down, and what moved Marija Skrinjaric to follow her father on his journey to faith yet prevented her getting waylaid? Why did Emily Mitchell go on the camp?

the unpredictable Spirit

We can only speculate on the answers to such questions. The mystery of the moving of the Spirit of God, essential for coming to the Father, is beyond our understanding. The miracle of lives transformed is God's domain not ours. However, without losing sight of that miracle, some truths emerge.

Christian teaching in childhood

Millions receive some kind of early Christian teaching that does not lead them to a Christian life, but we can still see that when gospel stories are learned early on, their truths echo, however faintly, for a lifetime.

Ron Tevita's and John Langham's families were always linked to the church, Charlie Farmery and Andrew Ramsbottom had Sunday School teaching for years, Tarsh Koia and Annette Bailey were taught religious education in school. Annette had Sunday School which grew into church. The degree and the impact of their Christian teaching varied, but in each case, some kind of on-going Christian education developed. Some young people without any Christian background do have a 'Damascus Road' experience, but it appears not to be the norm.

key relationships and prayer

The Christian background need not be large to be effective. Tarsh Koia is an encouraging example of a person with tenuous links to Christianity who nevertheless hung onto every one, as are Graham Eagle and Annette Bailey. They used the little knowledge they had as a basis for seeking more. Rene Galbes appears to have been less intentional about his faith journey but having begun, he built on this narrow base. Some drew on a Christian heritage of which they were largely unaware-like Tarsh's great grandmother who 'always prayed for all her mokopuna'. Annette's godmother was a woman of prayer, Graham's grandfather wrote poetry about God and was the son of a minister. Andrew Ramsbottom's and Charlie Farmery's families took them to church, as did Ron Tevita's. Andrew's grandparents prayed for him, and Marija Skrinjaric's father must have prayed for Marija. Rene Galbes tells us that people in his church began to pray for him while Iris Lee went to church with her family when they discovered a Christian faith.

We will never know who else prayed for these people, but it seems that various people did. Katie de Veau and Bren must have prayed for Emily Mitchell and Adele Ross, the Hyatts for Charlie Farmery, Martin Yeoman for Graham Eagle, Emblem and Wyper for Wayne Dixon, Gina Wong's brother and his friends for Gina, and Gary Colville for Ron Tevita. Prayer has powerful results.

on going group learning

Some on-going form of Christian education is common to every story here, be it church or youth group, special study groups or school Christian groups. Whether they were personal sharing times with another person or something else, every one benefited from some form of ongoing Christian learning. It would be hard to differentiate whether this led them into faith or resulted in faith growing.

Two recurring and often overlapping factors appear to have enabled this Christian learning:

- an ongoing interest from someone they knew
- opportunity to become part of a group they found attractive

A group, or a person in a group appear to be vital assistants in developing faith. For Annette Bailey, the group was her Sunday school, Graham Eagle's was at school while for Rene Galbes, it was a friend who first led him into the Bible and then on to a church. Gina Wong admired her brother's friends and was glad to be part of their group, John Langham's sister encouraged him toward ISCF, Ron Tevita sang and danced with JAM, Charlie Farmery benefited from the Pathfinders and their leaders. For Adele Ross, it was found in a dance group and a church, for Marija Skrinjaric through a church and some missionaries, while Emily Mitchell was inspired by Katie de Veau. Andrew Ramsbottom was encouraged in his Bible reading by Miss Preller, Wayne Dixon by the leaders of his youth club and Tarsh Koia found the university Christian Fellowship extremely helpful when she joined it as a young Christian.

specific deliberate challenge

Few of these people grew to make an act of Christian commitment without responding to a specific, deliberate challenge. Moving by stages, advancing in different degrees, some discovered their spirit responded to God before they even found the words to explain what was happening. A common feature is their recall of a time when the gospel was spelled out to them in clear terms, when they were asked, 'Well, what about it?' and they responded. Some situations were personal, others group-related. The degree of drama or publicity varied. For some there was more than one moment, with each occasion bringing a new level of commitment. Some of the young people had little understanding, responding more by will and heart than by head. All found it useful when someone else drew together the threads of the pattern they had been following.

Others actually responded to earlier events. Ron Tevita chose a day when his pastor offered prayer for those wishing to go to the front of the church because 'This is the day I state it.' John Langham acknowledges his confirmation classes as critical. For Adele Ross, clear teaching at camp brought together what she had already learned. After 'no special occasion', she came away with clarity regarding her faith. Emily Mitchell made her commitment after a camp also, and deliberately filled in a response coupon in a Gideon Bible. She was on her own, responding to a challenge written in the book. Marija Skrinjaric's father asked her what she made of God. Gina Wong was asked by her brother, Rene Galbes, Iris Lee and Annette Bailey, by their respective pastors.

Annette also responded to an invitation from a missionary at a meeting and it seems that various meetings have played a role in the lives of many of the young people. For instance, Wayne Dixon responded silently in response to a general question about commitment; Andrew Ramsbottom made two significant responses after meetings at different stages in his development; Charlie Farmery responded to a challenge during a camp. The catalyst for Graham Eagle was a pastor who unexpectedly visited his home, seemingly out of nowhere. In effect the pastor said, 'You need this,' then followed him up frequently at church.

Christian camps

Another significant recurring theme is the role of camps. Obviously, you do not have to go to a camp to become a Christian, but for Charlie and Graham, Andrew, Wayne and Annette, Marija, Adele, Emily, John and Iris, the temporary community was immensely helpful in one way or another. Depending on how we define 'temporary community', we could add Ron and Rene as well, and probably Gina and Tarsh. Camps are times when role models are accessible, teaching can be given and heard in a peer group both admired and enjoyed. They can be powerful times for allowing the gospel to be heard and for a response to be made.

involvement in service

It is said that people identify most vigorously with a cause when they are allowed to have a stake in that cause. All fourteen people in these stories tell of some kind of Christian involvement that made them feel useful. Annette Bailey and Wayne Dixon helped lead Christian groups at their high schools, and so did John

Langham; Adele Ross and Ron Tevita were part of performing groups; Rene Galbes worked with members of his family; Graham Eagle moved very early into youth work; Emily Mitchell and Andrew Ramsbottom became camp leaders; Tarsh Koia and Charlie Farmery led small groups on their university campuses; Marija Skrinjaric found a place in a nearby mission team and then in a local fellowship, Gina Wong and Iris Lee both accepted responsibility with the Overseas Christian Fellowship and Iris, as a child, felt useful in her local church as each week she helped put the school room into order for the church meeting.

conclusions

So, what can we learn from these people who have let us have a view into their lives? Hopefully you have formed some conclusions of your own by this stage, but here are some that stand out:

- Adolescence is a fruitful time for the gospel
- No adolescent comes from a spiritual vacuum
- They respond to care, love and loyalty
- Consistent Christian teaching with a clear challenge brings results
- Helpful peer groups and role models they admire, especially close and caring friends, are formative
- Biblical input when linked to prayer has great power

We can only speculate on the wonder of seeing the movement of the Spirit of God in power. If we accept adolescents, love and listen to them, challenge them and give them something to do in the context of helpful peer groups with praying friends, we cannot guarantee their salvation, but what we will have done is to 'allow the children to come to me.'

Of such is the kingdom of heaven.